What Others Are Saying

"This fantastic devotional by Crystal Lowery is perfect for the busy person, like a businessman once told me that he struggled to know how to be intimate with the Lord. So, in gatherings, he explained, 'I often attach myself to the prayers I hear being prayed so I can quickly feel God's love for me and my love for Him.' Crystal's devotional, *Sweet Love Letters to Jesus* is ready-made for you and me to add our 'yes' and 'amen' to hers as she reaches for His throne. As Crystal records her daily devotional praying to the Lord, we can easily add or attach ourselves to hers, and experience and express our love for God. This is my kind of devotional—one that draws us into His presence. Get this devotional and while you're at it, buy one as a gift for a friend!"

-- Steve Shultz
Founder, and President, *The Elijah List* and *Elijah Streams TV*

"Having experienced traumatic loss, in the death of her husband, Crystal was faced with the decision to hold on to her faith though her prayer for her husband to be healed was not answered the way that she had hoped. It was during that season of needing answers to very real questions that she spent hours seeking the Lord. From her time in His presence, grace and peace were poured into her, and a new depth of love for her Savior and Lord emerged.

Much like the biblical story of Ruth, Crystal's decision to follow God's plan and trust His purpose, despite her loss, brought a love for her 'Boaz,' the Lord Jesus, which is eloquently reflected in these *Sweet Love Letters to Jesus*. I am pleased to refer her Psalms-like writings based on the Word of God to you."

-- Jim Cernero
Revivalist, Pastor, Author, Healing, and Worship Minister www.jimcernero.org

"Crystal has captured the true heart of Bridal Love. Every prayer, every intimate expression of her communion with the Lord burns with the flame of love! Every page bears a divine branding of the marks and scars of her heart."

-- Pastor Theo Koulianos, Sr.
Jesus Center

"We all know that amid our greatest suffering, God is the closest to us! These *Sweet Love Letters to Jesus* came straight from Crystal's heart during her most difficult season, having lost her beloved husband. We highly recommend this devotional. The Holy Spirit will draw you into a more intimate relationship with Jesus."

-- Apostles Kiril and Angelina Istatkov
Kiril Istatkov Ministries, Charleston, SC

"Crystal has written a different kind of devotional. Putting words to what we all think, she has truly written as the title suggests, love letters to her Lord.

Endearing and uplifting, her book is a unique addition to your biblical library."

-- Chuck Girard
CCM Art8st

"The very depth of Crystal's heart and her relationship with her Heavenly Father, are so well expressed by evocative, defined, and detailed words; I am immediately shown the way to my Heavenly Father, His Son Jesus, and the Holy Spirit. The more I read *Sweet Love Letters to Jesus*, the more the message becomes real to my heart. They are so concentrated that I took my time weighing each sentence, each word. Many times, I found myself pondering the only person that mattered in the moment, the Lord Jesus Christ. It is impossible to read them without entering His presence.

At one point, I started to read out loud (something I would recommend you do), and I experienced an even deeper, more personal relationship with the person of Jesus.

Sweet Love Letters to Jesus made me cry, sing, and meditate on His love for me and our world. Thank you, Crystal, for your obedience to the Father in these writings, and making yourself vulnerable in such a personal way.

Allow these modern-day psalms to usher you into a more personal relationship with the Heavenly Father.

-- Liliane G.H. (Rood) Vernaud
Missionary pastor to the *Democratic Republic of Congo*

Sweet Love Letters to Jesus

Your 90-Day Journey of Intimacy with Jesus

CRYSTAL G.H. LOWERY

www.WorldwidePublishingGroup.com
7710-T Cherry Park Dr, Ste 224
Houston, Texas 77095
(713) 766-4271

Cover photo by Teeography, www.Teeography.com

ISBN: 978-1-68411-855-7

FOREWORD

I wholeheartedly recommend this 90-day journey to everyone who seeks the highest prize in life. Cultivating a deep intimate life with Jesus Christ is the pinnacle to all of life's existence. In this three-month experience, Crystal will guide you into the greatest encounter of all; falling intensely in love with Love Himself. Crystal is one of the most humble, authentic, and genuine Jesus lovers in this current day and age that God is raising in such a profound way to touch the nations of the world. What I so admire and honor about Crystal is that she walks in the very manuscript written before you. She has learned how to skate through both life's trials and victories from the place of eternal embrace. Crystal lives a life of union with Jesus Christ the Bridegroom King. This Spirit breathed guide is certain to transform your life forever and leave you marked by Love Divine.

Brian Guerin, Founding President

Bridal Glory International

FOREWORD

When I first met Crystal Lowery, I knew there was something different, so extraordinary about this woman's heart. She not only carried a radiance of God's love, but there was an innocence on her face and in her faith that caused me to take a deep breath. We effortlessly shared our journeys and the encounters with God's love that had changed our lives.

She shared her desire to publish a book that she was writing titled, "Sweet Love Letters to Jesus". I was thrilled because it was obvious to me, the well of her soul was deep with life changing truths.

Today, the church and the world are inundated with "Self Help" books. Fans will always choose knowledge, while followers embrace intimacy. We need to be careful to never allow the *knowledge of God* to replace *intimacy with God*. We have created a system focused around learning, our default setting is knowledge, and not intimacy. Now, please don't get me wrong, studying and learning from God's Word is invaluable. Jesus Himself, referenced, read, and quoted all kinds of passages from the Old Testament, ample proof that He had studied God's Word with great care and diligence.

However, we can't expect knowledge to replace intimacy, even though we often try to. And I think we try to substitute knowledge for intimacy because knowledge is so much easier. It's easy for us to say, "Well, I know about Jesus," but He wants to know us.

In "Sweet Love Letters to Jesus," Crystal makes herself vulnerable, opening up about her hunger to know and be made known. She allows us a sneak peek into her heart's devotion, as she longs after God's heart.

I am reminded of Simon the Pharisee in Luke 7. He knew a lot about Jesus and his teachings and wanted to learn more. He calls him "teacher", it tells me he's most interested in learning from Jesus, but not open to Jesus. But there is a woman in the story who didn't come to know Him as a teacher, but as the lover of her soul.

Simon sees all this woman does for Jesus, her embarrassing actions, and the Bible tells us, *"When the Pharisee who had invited Jesus saw this, he said to himself, 'If this man were a prophet, he would know who is touching him and what kind of woman she is—that she is a sinner.'"* (Luke 7:39) Jesus knowing Simon's thoughts, answered, *"Look, I came in the house. You did not give me a kiss, not even on my hand. She hasn't stopped kissing my feet. You gave me nothing to wash my feet with, and she is washing my feet with her tears. You gave me no olive oil for my head; she has poured perfume on my feet."*

And people can just see the brokenness of this woman, and then Jesus turns to this woman and He says, "Your sins are forgiven. Go in peace." Simon brought Jesus to the meal, but all he wanted was knowledge. He wanted to keep things shallow, and he defined his relationship by not washing Christ's feet, not caring to kiss him, not being willing to anoint his head, but this woman was willing to open her heart to Jesus. Thank you, Crystal, for making yourself vulnerable and for being open and allowing Jesus to touch your life, so He can touch mine and countless others.

Crystal, you my friend are an ambassador of His love, your heart has impacted my life. Thank you for writing "Sweet Love Letters to Jesus" to benefit my journey with God. Now, I am ready to write my own, because of YOU!

Pastor Sam Hinn, *The Gathering Place*

DAY 1

Thank you, Jesus, for loving me beyond my ability to comprehend. You are my only source. Only you can truly satisfy me. You know me - everything about me! You knew me before I was born. You set me apart. You give me a purpose. You make all my empty places overflow and smooth my rough parts. You make my crooked places straight. You make rivers for me in areas of desert. You satisfy all my needs and give me the desires of my heart. You surprise me beyond what I can ask or think. I am so grateful. I love you because of who you are. I set all my adoration on you. I love that I am yours and that you are mine. I don't want it any other way. I'm so in love with you.

Song of Solomon 3:16 (KJV): *"My beloved is mine, and I am his..."*

DAY 2

I have fallen in love with you, the sweetest song of all the ages. You sing to me and over me. Your melody envelops my life, my soul, and my spirit. Your voice is the sound of rushing waters. I would give my life to hear your voice because I love the music. I love the words you speak. Your words in a melody are eternal bliss for my lovesick soul. You are my Love. I was the joy set before you – the prize of your suffering and sacrifice. The song you sing is about me.

Song of Solomon 2:1 (TPT) – *"I am truly his rose, the very theme of his song. I'm overshadowed by his love growing in the valley!"*

DAY 3

Thank you that we can be one in spirit. Thank you that this oneness flows into my soul and body. I am in you, and you are in me. As I look to you, all I see is you and not myself. I fade away, and I only see you. I have become the Shulamite in Song of Solomon, the feminine form of the same word used for Solomon, the bridegroom. How powerful this is when I think about oneness. We are two but have become one. Let your presence wash over me and saturate me. Infuse me with yourself. Thank you for loving me.

1 Corinthians 6:17 (TPT) – *"But the one who joins himself to the Lord is mingled into one spirit with him."*

A Passion Translation Footnote – "In Song of Songs, the word for *Shulamite* and the word for *Solomon* are taken from the same Hebrew root word. One is masculine, and the other is feminine. The name Solomon occurs seven times in the book, which points us to the perfect King, Jesus Christ. We are one spirit with our King, united with him. You have become the Shulamite."

DAY 4

Thank you, Jesus, for invading this space. Thank you for invading my life and searching for me. You chase me no matter where I go. You are always where I am. I want to be where you are. I desire to know you in fullness in every part of myself and my life. I don't want to take another step without you or take another breath without you. You are my very breath. The steps that I take are a path you have laid for me, steps of where you have been, and where you are going. Our footprints are incorporated together to form a beautiful tapestry. What a lovely piece of art, to look upon this tapestry, the path of our unity. The fabric is woven in and out, representing our journey together. Thank you for your love and grace and beauty. I am confident that the finished tapestry will be beyond my ability to comprehend, but I am willing, and my desire is to continue being woven together with you. I know the best is yet to come!

Song of Songs 1:5 (TPT) – "...*Yet you are so lovely – like the fine linen tapestry hanging in the Holy Place.*"

Day 5

I love you, Jesus. I give you all of myself. I give you this day, this week, this month, and this year. I give you my present, my past, and my future. Transform me into a reflection of you. Take away the rough, scratchy places in me. Remove the ugly spots. Let your light shine through me. Radiate through me. Illuminate through me. Darkness cannot exist where you are. Use me as a person to magnify you. I want to be your magnifying glass. Shine through me. Holy Spirit speak through me today to magnify and glorify Jesus. I love you more today than ever before. I want to know your love for me. Help me to understand. Reveal yourself to me like fresh and new ways. I love you.

James 4:7 (NCV) – *"So give yourselves completely to God…"*

DAY 6

Thank you, Jesus, for loving me. I am the center of the romance story of the ages. God, you proved your love to me by giving Jesus as a gift so that I can be redeemed from the curse. I am redeemed from sickness, poverty, debt, lack, death, and every bad thing brought into the earth by the curse. Instead, I have health, wealth, debt freedom, abundance, life, and every good thing that you have provided for me. Thank you that you loved me so much to do this. I thank you for every blessing in my life. I know that you are the source of all goodness in my life. I love you. Thank you for loving me. The price you paid was so abundantly perfect, and so how can I not adore you? Deepen my passion for you. Deepen my love for you. Help me to know love by how you are love. You are love itself. Break down every wall of limitation around my understanding of love. I allow love to invade me. I allow you to invade me. I love you.

John 3:16 (TPT) — *"For this is how much God loved the world — he gave his one and only, unique Son as a gift. So now everyone who believes in him will never perish but experience everlasting life."*

DAY 7

Thank you, Jesus, for changing my seasons. Thank you for newness and freshness. Thank you that you bring change into my life. Thank you that you have orchestrated behind the scenes for me, and the result is overwhelming to my soul. No matter my efforts, they fall short in comparison to the magnificent creativity and thought and love that you have poured into my future. You have already been in my future just like you have been in my past and my present. You are in all these places right now. You are victorious over all circumstances and things. The barrenness that was in my last season is now gone, and I enter the garden of fruitfulness and plenty and joy. Thank you that you have prepared such wonderful things for me. I stand in amazement at your power and am in such awe of you. My heart cannot contain the love I have for you. I am so thankful and full of love.

Song of Songs 2:11 (TPT) – *"The season has changed, the bondage of your barren winter has ended, and the season of hiding is over and gone…"*

DAY 8

I love you, Jesus. There is no one like you. I worship you because of who you are. I wait in absolute stillness and silence before you. I am confident that you will rescue me from my current situation. My only hope and all my expectation rest in you. I take comfort knowing that you have never let me down. Not once have you failed me. Even in my humanness, you cover me with your grace. The oil of your grace is continually flowing and covering all of me. Thank you for giving me peace beyond my understanding. I will wait in absolute stillness as long as it takes for you to rescue me because I am in standing in the presence of the One I love. I love you, Jesus.

Psalm 62:5 (TPT) – *"I am standing in absolute stillness, silent before the one I love, waiting as long as it takes for him to rescue me. Only God is my Savior, and he will not fail me."*

DAY 9

Jesus, how I love you. I want your presence. Be with me and show me your face. I know that you are with me always. I long for the day when I can see you continually. I dream about being in heaven with you – in the city of bliss. One of my favorite hymns is *Amazing Grace*, and even though I want to saturate myself with the words of the entire song, I believe my favorite verse is the last one.

"When we've been there ten thousand years,

Bright shining as the sun,

We've no less days to sing God's praise

Than when we first begun."

Until that time, let it be on earth as it is in heaven. Let your glory come. Let your presence come. I ache to be in your presence. I desire to sing in duet with you, a divine duet, about our love for each other. I thirst for you; I am coming to you; I am running to you.

Revelation 22:17 (TPT) – *"'Come,' says the Holy Spirit and the Bride in divine duet. Let everyone who hears this duet join them in saying, "Come." Let everyone gripped with spiritual thirst say, "Come," and let everyone who craves the gift of living water come and drink it freely. 'It is my gift to you! Come.'"*

DAY 10

Jesus, I love you. I love everything about you. I love the words you speak. I love your Word. You are the Word. Because I love you, I love everything you say. I love each word and all of them together. I love their sound. I love their meaning. I love to speak your words. I agree with your words. I continually, day and night, put your words before me. I cherish what you say. What you say is who you are. You are equal to the Word because you are one and the same. When I speak the word, I am speaking to you. Every cell of my body stands at attention and honors and respects the authority and dominion it commands. In every situation in my life, your word covers. In all my circumstances, your word is controlling. Your word always comes to pass. It is infallible, it is all-knowing, it is completely authoritative, and it is not subject to anything else.

Your word is your equivalent. As I saturate myself, and I soak myself in your word, I know you better and deeper and more intimately. Your word brings me life where there was death. Your word brings me hope when there was nothing but doubt. Your word gives me hope and a future where there was a pit and an ending. Your word is my life. It feeds my soul. It feeds me; It is alive; It is sharper than any weapon. It is more powerful than anything that can come against it. Thank you, Jesus, that you are the Word. Your word is above all other words. I enter into an agreement with you Jesus when I speak your Word. You are my pleasure and my passion. You are my life: you, only you, just you.

Psalm 1: 2 (TPT) – *"His pleasure and passion are remaining true to the Word of "I Am," meditating day and night in the true revelation of light."*

Day 11

I am in such awe of you Jesus. You constantly amaze me. As I know you deeper and deeper, you reveal more of who you are to me. In my finite mind, I wonder why you don't reveal all of yourself to me now. I know that I would not be able to comprehend the richness and highest form of all there is by the limited capacity of my soul. As I grow into whom you have made me to be, I desire to know you in that fullness and intimacy. You are the beginning of all and the end of all. You are everything in the middle. You are the Aleph and the Tav, the Alpha and the Omega, the A and the Z. You are all the letters in between. You are the sum of all the letters. You are the Word. I speak the Word. I speak You. Be alive in me. Be overflowing from my lips. Let my words be pleasing to you. I only want to speak what my Father says. You are everything to me. You amaze me. I love you with a fierceness that consumes me.

Revelation 1:8 (TPT) – *"I am the Aleph and the Tav, the beginning and the ending…"*

A Passion Translation Footnote – "Jesus affirms he has all knowledge and is the sum of all truth. Not only is he all the letters, he is also everything the letters can convey."

Day 12

Jesus, I love you. You are my focus, my desire, and my longing. Reveal yourself to me in new ways. Thank you for our personal relationship and the time we have together. I love how you speak to me. I love all your words. I love your voice. Whatever you say to me, I cherish and hold tightly. The secrets we have are too precious to share. I love having secrets that are only between us. I continually feast on the hidden manna – your words and yourself in my heart. Thank you that you are always giving yourself to me. Thank you that you give all of yourself to me. I want to give all of myself to you. Thank you for a new name that is only for me to know. I love that you are all powerful and yet so wonderfully personal to me. I love you beyond what my words can express.

Revelation 2:17 (TPT) – *"…To everyone who is victorious, I will let him feast on the hidden manna and give him a shining white stone. And written upon the white stone is inscribed his new name, known only to the one who receives it."*

A Passion Translation Footnote – "We see that there are personal mysteries imparted to God's people, that is, secrets that are between the believer and Jesus. Only someone devoted to God is to know the meaning of the shining white stone and the name written upon it."

13

Day 13

How I thank you, Jesus, that you have provided a way for me to be like you. Thank you that you reveal yourself to me. Thank you that my eyes are open to see you. Thank you that all religious bondage is broken, and the chains have fallen. I thank you that because of my freedom, I can run to you and be transformed into your likeness. I want to be one of your fiery red ones, identifiable by your blood over my life. I am marked by you and am forever set apart. I want to be what you say I am. Thank you that I am precious and valuable and priceless before you – a red fiery burning jewel – in love with you.

Revelation 3:1 (TPT) – *"Write the following to the messenger of the congregation in Sardis…"*

A Passion Translation Footnote – "Sardis can mean 'those who have escaped' or 'red ones' (jewels). How we need to escape every form of religious bondage on our journey into Christlikeness. By the blood of Christ, we are redeemed and set free to be his fiery (red) ones, like jewels before God. Twice in the history of Sardis it had fallen to its enemies because it was not alert and watching. It was conquered once in 549 BC by King Cyrus of Persia, and again in 214 BC by Antiochus the Great. For this reason, the people of Sardis were asleep and needed an awakening."

DAY 14

Thank you, Jesus, that you are you. There is no one like you. Thank you that you love me and want me to be your own. Thank you that I am on your heart day and night, with no end. Thank you that you gave yourself for me, a price so worthy and precious so that I can be your bride. I love that you have been standing at the door to my heart, knocking. There are no words to describe such love, for you are the very thing itself. You are so wonderful, so beautiful, and so full of all I need. I fully open the door of my heart to you. My answer is "Yes!" to you! I will be your bride. I desire to be your bride. I long to be your bride. Thank you, Jesus, my King Bridegroom. I love you.

Revelation 3:20 (TPT) – *"Behold, I'm standing at the door, knocking! If your heart is open to hearing my voice and you open the door within, I will come in to you and feast with you, and you will feast with me."*

Passion Translation Footnotes – "The Aramaic can be translated 'I have been standing at the door, knocking.' Jesus knocking on the door points us to the process of an ancient Jewish wedding invitation. In the days of Jesus, a bridegroom and his father would come to the door of the bride-to-be carrying the betrothal cup and the bride-price. Standing outside, they would knock. If she fully opened the door, she was saying 'Yes, I will be your bride.' Jesus and his father, in the same way, are knocking on the doors of our hearts, inviting us to be the bride of Christ."

"This is likely taken from Song of Solomon 5:1-2, where the king knocks on the door of the heart of the Shulamite, longing to come in and feast with her."

Day 15

Thank you, Jesus, for being with me today. I know you are right beside me, in front of me, and behind me, helping me and guiding me in every way. When I get busy and caught up in all the to-dos of each day, you are with me. When every person, it seems, needs something from me, you are there filling me up again. When I need energy, you provide. When I need rest, you remind me to enter into your perfect rest. When I feel like my life consists of endless chores and projects, you give me purpose. When I feel like I'm at the end, you remind me that I am the head and not the tail. When I feel pressure and stress, you take it away from me. When I am hungry, you feed me. Jesus, you are everything to me. You listen to me when I need someone to talk to. You speak to me when I need to hear. You help me right when I need it. You never leave me. Through all the good times and all the challenges, you are there. I am so desperate for you. All my attempts are so futile without you. I'm so glad you love me and care about me. You're my everything. All the time. I always need you more.

Hebrews 13:5 (TPT) – *"...For hasn't he promised you, 'I will never leave you alone, never! And I will not loosen my grip on your life!'"*

DAY 16

Jesus, how I love you. You are more precious to me today than ever before. I adore you, Jesus. You are so wonderful and worthy. Even all the angels bow down before you and kiss you in worship. I want to speak to you and hear you speak to me. I want to be silent and still and just be in your presence. I want your touch upon me! My desire for you deepens with each day and each passing moment. I grow and come to know just how much I need you. Be with me all the time, everywhere I go, in everything I do, and in everything I say. Let me be a brightness – a light reflecting your glory. I bow before you, I kiss you in worship, and I totally and completely worship and adore you.

Hebrews 1:6 (TPT) – "...'Let all my angels bow down before him and kiss him in worship.'"

A Passion Translation Footnote – "...The Greek word for worship, *proskuneo*, includes three concepts: 'to bow,' 'to kiss,' and 'to pay homage (worship)...'

DAY 17

Jesus, I give you my heart, my soul, and everything I am. I surrender all my desires, my wishes, and my goals to you. I want your plan for me. I thank you that you always love me with a fiery passion. Thank you that you judge whatever gets in the way of me being with you. I am your bride, and I want you. Thank you that you reached out and took hold of me. Thank you that you wanted me. Thank you that you loved me enough to pay such a price for me to be yours. Thank you that you are not moderately persuaded for me but fiercely passionate toward me. All I can do is respond to you with unrelenting arms that are open. Take me to be with you. I want not just to be with you, in your presence, but to know you fully. Let my love toward you be propelled by burning fire and passion which are swept together and ignited. You mesmerize me by our love story – the story you wrote before you created me to be your love.

Revelation 6:16 (TPT) – *"...Hide us quickly from the glorious face of the one seated on the throne and from the wrath of the Lamb..."*

A Passion Translation Footnote – "Few phrases in the Bible could seem more contradicting than 'the wrath [anger] of the Lamb' (not the anger of the Lion). This is corrective and redemptive – not beastly rage but passion to judge whatever gets in the way between the Lamb and his bride. The Greek word *'orge'* means 'to reach out with passionate desire and take hold of.' The simplest definition of the Greek word *'orge'* could be 'fiery passion.'"

DAY 18

Jesus, thank you for your overwhelming and compassionate love for me. Thank you that love itself is your very nature. It is you. You amaze me every day with your constant embrace, your never-ending kisses, and your sweet passionate desire for me. Thank you, Jesus, for sympathizing with me in my humanity. Thank you that you not only love me with all of yourself, but you are the Overcomer of everything that is fallen. You are my Conqueror. You are my Victor. You are my High-Priest. Because of this, I can freely and boldly approach the innermost holy place – the place where love is enthroned – to receive mercy's kiss and discover grace that I urgently need. My ship is in a storm. I need your grace now. Thank you that you are always with me. Thank you that as I approach your love, you strengthen me. You are my everything. I love you.

Hebrews 4:16 (TPT) – *"So now we come freely and boldly to where love is enthroned, to receive mercy's kiss and discover the grace we urgently need to strengthen us in our time of weakness."*

DAY 19

I love you and lift you high above everything, Jesus. You are the one who loves me. I sing about your love for me. Your love is faithful. You believe in me. Your love sustains me. Your love is poured over me continually, and it reaches my innermost places. Your love is so amazing, and I need your help to express what it is and all it is. I could sing of your love forever and still not exhaust what it means to me. Your love is never-ending. It is inexhaustible. It never runs out. It fills me up and overflows from me. Your love is a peaceful stream, and it is a powerful rushing waterfall. Your love is all things to me. It is everything I need. It is everything I want. It is all my hope and desire.

Your love gives me joy; Your love gives me hope; It gives me a purpose. I cannot hide from your love. I run freely toward your love and say, "I'm yours!" My eyes are always on you. You are the center of it all, my focus, my target. It is you that I love in return. My heart desires to love you even a fraction of how much you love me. I want my love for you to grow and expand. Can my love ever match yours? Your love is beautiful. It is perfect. Thank you that you have always loved me. Thank you that you will always love me. I continually run to you.

Psalm 101:1 (TPT) – *"Lord, I will sing about your faithful love for me. My song of praise will have your justice as its theme."*

DAY 20

I am continually amazed at the truth you continually reveal to me. I can read your Word and you speak to me. Thank you, Jesus, for being the Word. Thank you for speaking to me. Thank you that I am your bride. Thank you that as your bride, I am the increase of you as your counterpart. Only you would create such a relationship and design it perfectly. I am the one you love, and you wholly gave yourself for me. I was the joy set before you. Through all of the pain and suffering that I cannot even imagine, you did it for me. Even more, you did it for my increase. I am your counterpart, and I am completed by you.

Everything I lack, you have. Everything I need, you have. All my needs, you provide; All my desires, you grant; All my tears, you wipe away. You increase me in every way. I am your glory. I am your joy, but you are my glory and the fullness of my joy. I am dizzy from the concept of our love for each other. I am the one you love, and you put me in front of you as your reward. You are so good to me. You are always good. You are always kind. You are always loving. My words cannot express my gratitude and thankfulness to you. All I can do is simply tell you that I completely and fully love you too.

John 3:30 (TPT) – *"So it's necessary for him to increase and for me to be diminished."*

A Passion Translation Footnote – "The increase of Christ in v.30 is the bride of Christ in v.29. We are the increase of Christ as his counterpart. Just as Eve was the increase of Adam, the bride is the increase of Christ on the earth."

DAY 21

Jesus, you are perfect. You are wonderful. You are lovely. You are beautiful. You have a perfect place for me next to you. I want to dwell with you and live next to you in your shining place of glory. Thank you for allowing me access to dwell and make a habitat for my life in this sanctuary, this shining place of glory. I dare to dwell with you. Let it be me. I long to dwell with you. I only want to be in your presence, with your precious glory radiating on me for all eternity. I draw close to you. I seek your face. I seek your presence. Shine on me holy Jesus, my absolute everything. I cannot bear to be without the benefit of being in the place so close and tucked next to you, a place you have prepared for me since the beginning. There is everything I need before me, next to me, and shining on me. You are very much alive within me, for I have let you into my innermost places, and there I have also provided a place for you to dwell. What a privilege of being close to you, to have such access and opportunity to live next to you in such an indescribable place, a shining place of glory.

Psalm 15:1 (TPT) – *"Lord, who dares to dwell with you? Who presumes the privilege of being close to you, living next to you in your shining place of glory?"*

Passion Translation Footnotes – "…It is a song that reveals who will dwell in God's holy presence and who will live with him in heaven's glory. It actually is a description of Zion's perfect Man, Christ Jesus and all those who are transformed into his image…"

"…The Hebrew word for 'sanctuary' is taken from a root word for 'shining place.'"

Day 22

I'm so much in awe of you. In every way possible, you are perfect in yourself, in your creation, in your plan. I put my faith in you. I put all my trust in you and you alone. I am convinced that as each day passes, you have every detail of my life worked out for my benefit. I stay in your presence where I long to be. I listen to you and hear what you speak. I obey you. This is my heart's desire. I know that you lead me and are weaving a wonderful tapestry of details together which ultimately is for my good. I know that you have called me and have designed a purpose for me. This is your reason for creating me. As I dwell with you in the secret chambers, I am transformed into your likeness, Jesus. You put your mark upon me. I am forever sealed. Just as a bride wearing a ring, I am marked visibly and physically for you. I am marked in my soul and my spirit. I am sealed with a seal that cannot be broken. I am unapologetically yours.

Romans 8:28-29 (TPT) – "*So we are convinced that every detail of our lives is continually woven together to fit into God's perfect plan of bringing good into our lives, for we are his lovers who have been called to fulfill his designed purpose. For he knew all about us before we were born, and he destined us from the beginning to share the likeness of his Son.*"

A Passion Translation Footnote – "…The Aramaic can be translated 'sealed us' (with God's mark upon us)…"

DAY 23

Thank you, Jesus, for being the one at the very center of the Throne of God. You are the victorious one, the overcoming one, the radiant one. Only you can flawlessly guide me and be my path for life. As I set my eyes on you, you lead me. As I gaze at your beauty, you lift me. As I marvel at your wonder, you satisfy me. You make all my rocky paths smooth. Your voice is soothing to my soul. Your words are like a salve for my wounds. You continuously shepherd me. You bring me to everlasting fountains of the water of life, for you are the very thing itself. You are life itself. Thank you that you wipe all my tears away. You anoint all my tears and turn them into joy. As you wipe them away, they are replaced with joy and gladness. Anoint me, Jesus. Anoint not just my tears, but my very life itself. I pursue you. I wait on you. Search my heart and know how much I love you.

Revelation 7:17 (TPT) — *"For the Lamb at the center of the throne continuously shepherds them unto life — guiding them to the everlasting fountains of the water of life. And God will wipe from their eyes every last tear!"*

Passion Translation Footnotes — "...As translated from the Aramaic. The sacrificial heart of Christ as the Lamb will guide them and be their path of life."

"The Greek word for 'anoint' is 'to wipe' or 'smear.' It is possible to translate this "He will anoint every tear shed from their eyes..."

27

DAY 24

Jesus, to see you with my eyes, to behold your beauty, what a privilege and honor it is for me to look upon your face. The power and love that radiate from your eyes are so pure and so true. Your gaze cuts through to my heart. My soul is suspended in anticipation of just a word from you. All my expectation is in you. May I dwell in the secret place, so close to you that I can feel your touch. I crave the moment I can touch you. At that moment, I am convinced I will know your heart, what motivates you, and what drives you. I desire to pluck the strings of your heart and hear the beautiful melody, a sweet and precious melody, a melody of truth and love. This is a melody which has always been and always will be. Timeless in character. Absolute in quality. The sound of the Living Expression of God.

1 John 1:1 (TPT) – *"We saw him with our very own eyes. We gazed upon him and heard him speak. Our hands touched him, the one who was from the beginning, the Living Expression of God."*

A Passion Translation Footnote – "The word for 'touch' is poetic. It comes from a sensory verb meaning 'to pluck the strings of an instrument.' It can also be translated 'to feel' … It is a though John is saying, 'We have plucked the chords of his being and felt what motivated him, his melody within.'"

DAY 25

Jesus, how can I even express my love to you? Can I even comprehend the magnitude of what my love should be for you? Expand my capacity to love you fully and completely and wholly. You know my heart. You created me. I am here to love you. How could you focus on me and endure the complete and utter agony of the cross? How could I be the joy set before you? I don't understand how such love can exist. How can such love be for me? In the recesses of my mind, I am still unable to imagine or contain such fullness. Help me to take in and be filled with your love – with you.

Thank you that you thought nothing of all the horrid shame, the utter humiliation you endured, along with all the pain and torment. I'm still learning of the scope and depth of your love. It will take a lifetime of discovering and growing in the knowledge of your love. I can hardly contain my expectation of the journey. With the intensity that I know and feel now, I dare to ask for more. Let the bliss which you intended be the result of me being the joy set before you and now with me always having you before me. At this juncture, at this crossing, we will see each other and be face to face. Let this moment be. Let this endure forever. All I can see is love before me.

Hebrews 12:2 (TPT) – "*...Because his heart was focused on the joy of knowing that you would be his, he endured the agony of the cross and conquered its humiliation, and now sits exalted at the right hand of the throne of God!*"

Passion Translation Footnotes – "This was the joy of our salvation. He placed before his eyes the bliss we would forever share with him, which empowered him to go through his agony." "As translated from the Aramaic. The Greek is 'thinking nothing of its shame.'"

DAY 26

Jesus, today I love you more than ever before. Thank you that you have caused my capacity to love to grow and expand. Let this continue as I receive layer upon layer of revelation from you. I am constantly filled by you. I am completed by you. Everything I lack, you provide. Everything I need, you make available. Your love is never-ending. As I continually go deeper and deeper in your love, you complete me. The beauty and mystery of your ways are that at the same time, I complete and fill you. I am humbled and recognize that your ways are so much better than mine. Everything you design is so perfect and purposeful. Thank you that you love me. I give you all of myself and ask you to help me love you in such a way and in such depth that is pleasing to you.

Ephesians 1:23 (TPT) – *"And now we, his church, are his body on the earth and that which fills him who is being filled by it!"*

A Passion Translation Footnote – "That is, as we are those who are filled (completed) by Christ, we also complete (fill) him. What a wonderful and humbling mystery is revealed by this verse."

DAY 27

Another day has come, Jesus. I have great expectations today of seeing your face. I want to memorize all the features of your face. I see your eyes and how they look at me. They are piercing and all-knowing, but somehow embrace me perfectly, full of love. I could look into your eyes for all of eternity and never do anything else. As you look back into my eyes, I know that you see into my soul and the longing I have to love you. I tell you this every day, but with each day that comes, the yearning intensifies. I have a fire burning on the inside of me that is blazing. Nothing will be able to extinguish these burning flames I carry within me.

You alone are my source of water, and only your water can satisfy me.

I desperately need to see your face. Reveal yourself to me. My life is open to you. I willingly lay everything before you to serve you. Lead me every step of the way, and I will obediently follow wherever you show me. Your footsteps are before me, and I put my feet into the molded prints where your feet have been – guiding me and showing me the perfect path. As I serve and love you, I constantly see your face. I have nowhere else to look because you are always before me. I am yours. You have been marked for me by your stripes. Now, mark me with your love. I am set apart for you and you alone.

Revelation 22:3 (TPT) – *"...His loving servants will serve him; they will constantly see his face, and his name will be on their foreheads."*

DAY 28

Jesus, I thank you that you have given me another day to love you. I am so grateful to you for who you are. You are what I set my eyes upon. You are what I set my affections on. You are the treasure of my heart. I know that I am special to you, that I am set apart for you, and that your love for me is so intense, so eternal, that I can never fully understand it with my mind. Your love is so unchanging. It is not based on your feelings toward me or what I do or accomplish. Your love will never diminish or fail to exist.

For all of eternity, your love is for me. I fall more in love with you every day as I try to comprehend your love for me, as I run to gaze into your eyes and as I never want to leave the private, secret place created just for me to enjoy. I love being so close to you. I ask God to show me your face daily. I know that when I see you, I see the Father. What a mystery, but what a beautiful mystery. I rest under the shadow of your wings, the wings of the cherubim that surround you. Thank you for revealing secrets to me. I feast continually on revelations of your covenant with me, promises that are so wonderful, so beautiful, and so precious to me. I never want to leave your side. I never want to leave your presence. I want to know you. I want to love you more and more.

Psalm 25:14 (TPT) – *"There's a private place reserved for the lovers of God, where they sit near him and receive the revelation – secrets of his promises."*

A Passion Translation Footnote – "Or 'covenant.'"

33

DAY 29

Jesus, you have captivated me. You have my soul. You have my heart. Your love has taken me and captured me. I passionately pursue you. This is my highest hope, my ultimate prize, my reward. I want to be with you. My passion rests in your love. The desperate need I have to be with you is met in your presence. I know that in your presence I have you. All of you. Just for myself. I am bonded to you. I love you so much there is nothing I can do with my love that will satisfy besides just being with you. My love has created a deep and emotional bond to you that is unbreakable. I am forever with you, never to be apart. For all of eternity, I am yours. I long to be with you and embrace you. I need your touch. Your embrace gives me strength and power. It is the fuel for my existence. I cannot go on without it. I don't want your embrace to end because you are the One I want. You are my love.

Psalm 18:1 (TPT) – *"Lord, I passionately love you, and I'm bonded to you, for now, you've become my power!"*

A Passion Translation Footnote – "David doesn't employ the common Hebrew word for 'love,' *'ahav,* but instead uses the Hebrew word for 'pity' or 'mercy.' How could David have mercy for God? The word he uses, *raham,* is the word used for a mother who loves and pities her child so much it manifests with a deep love and emotional bond. This concept, although difficult to convey in English, carries the thought of embrace and touch. It could actually be translated 'Lord, I want to hug you.' Haven't you ever felt like that?"

34

Day 30

My heart is beating in anticipation of being with you today. I love you, Jesus. I love everything about you. I love your name. Jesus. When I say your name, not only does all of heaven and earth stand at attention, but my heart leaps at the sound of the name of the one I love. Hem me in and besiege me, Jesus, from what is in my future and my past. You are above time. You created time, but it does not apply to you. You are the beginning and the end and all things in between. Thank you that you have already gone into my future and you know what is there.

You have a perfect plan for my future, and I will walk with you every step, but, because of your love for me, you are following behind to cover me from the place of my past. Your hand is always on me, and I must be close enough to touch you. Thank you for protecting my future from my past. Thank you for protecting me on the journey. Thank you that you surround me with a song of victory. You sing victory over me. You sing protection over me. You sing love over me. I cannot fathom the depths of your love for me, but I do know that I am with you and I am for you. My heart sings back to you in harmony - the epic love song of the ages.

Psalm 139:5 (TPT) — *"You've gone into my future to prepare the way, and in kindness, you follow behind me to spare me from the harm of my past. With your hand of love upon my life, you impart a blessing to me."*

A Passion Translation Footnote – "'You hem me in [lit., 'besiege me'] before and behind.' The implication is that God protects him from what may come in the future and what has happened in the past."

Day 31

Jesus, my soul is on its knees, bowed before you, asking for your presence. I know your presence is not a feeling or an emotion, but I can tell that my feelings and emotions are always affected by you – your closeness. My eyes are open and aware of evil strategies to interfere and steal my joy, but I will not allow a thief to take my joy. There are voids that I know exist in my life. They exist in my desires, in my dreams, and in my relationships. I know that you are the only one who can fill those barren places and make orchards grow where there once was a desert.

You have always existed, and you have always been. Everything finds completion in you. You complete me, and you fill me. You take away my hurts, my mourning and my feelings of lack. You love me with an incomprehensible love. I'm so glad you love me. I am nothing without you. You perfect me. You turn my ashes into beauty, and I am forever thankful for your love. Thank you for your presence. Thank you that you help me to love you when I need love the most. You're my everything. I love you.

Colossians 1:17 (TPT) – *"He existed before anything was made, and now everything finds completion in him."*

Day 32

Jesus, I love you. I love your presence. Your presence is you. When I want to escape, you are with me. When I want to hide, you are with me. When I wish I could forget myself, you are still with me. The darkest night cannot hide me. The lowest valley cannot conceal me. The deepest pit cannot contain me, because you are there. You draw me toward you. You chase me when I feel wonderful, and you pursue me when I feel miserable. You remind me of your constant presence. I can't go anywhere that is too far or too dark or too deep where you are not there with me.

Your love desires me. You bring light to my night. I am at the center of your thoughts, and your love focuses on me. How can I comprehend such love? I am so thankful for your love. I am so happy that you pursue me. I don't want to let my gratefulness diminish or my love be stagnant for you. Help me to grow and increase in your love so that I can love you more and more. Let there be no darkness, but only you, shining light into my soul. Shine love and penetrate my heart. I want to be completely yours.

Psalm 139:11 (TPT) – *"It's impossible to disappear from you or to ask the darkness to hide me, for your presence is everywhere, bringing light into my night."*

Day 33

Jesus, I woke up this morning with thoughts of you. As the sun's natural rays slowly came across the tops of the trees, I thanked you for another day. The beauty you have created for me today is overwhelming, but I look beyond the natural realm and fasten my gaze onto the one I love, the one my waking thoughts are about, and the one I wake up for. My eyes cannot be diverted to see anyone else. They are completely fastened to my Jesus. Like a grip, my gaze is focused and holding tightly to love set before me. I need you today. I need my eyes always to be looking at you. As I behold you, you fill my soul. You are the very existence of me. I live to be with you.

Hebrews 12:2 (TPT) – *"We look away from the natural realm, and we fasten our gaze onto Jesus..."*

DAY 34

Jesus, this morning you woke me tenderly to be with you. I felt you all around me. I am so thankful that each day, you are with me. As I sleep through the night, you watch me and smile. Daily, I never cease to be amazed at your infinite love for me. Every moment of my life you are thinking of me. You thought of me before I was born. You have thoughts and plans for me for all of eternity. When I think of the incalculable number of grains of sand in just a handful, I stagger to imagine the total number on earth. In trying to comprehend this almost impossible number, I know that your desires toward me are above and beyond the insurmountable quantity of sand on the seashores. How can it be possible? Your love is so intense, so deep, so vast, and so eternal that I fall to my knees and sit in utter stillness basking in who you are. You are so precious to me. You are the dearest thing to my heart. You are my very heart. I love you. Take my love and hold it in your heart, Jesus.

Psalm 139:17-18 (TPT) – *"Every single moment you are thinking of me! How precious and wonderful to consider that you cherish me constantly in your every thought! O God, your desires toward me are more than the grains of sand on every shore! When I awake each morning, you're still with me."*

Day 35

Jesus, you're the one I'm focused on today. I've given you my heart and my life – all of me. I continually give you all of myself. I examine myself as my worst critic because I don't want any part of my life to be withheld from you. If there is anything that I haven't fully given to you, let me see it. Reveal it to me. You know my heart. You know my desires. I live for you. I do everything for you. I breathe for you. You are my breath itself, my life, my purpose. I give myself wholly to you and subject myself to you. I give you full dominion over me. Pour down your love on me. Pour down yourself on me. Infuse me with your presence. Saturate me with knowing you. I'm yours. I'm a love-slave dedicated to you, loving you, obeying you, living for you, and giving my all to you. I don't want to be a slave to any other person or thing, just you. Only you. I love that I'm yours. I know that I'm yours. I know my identity. I'm yours, and you are mine. I'm all in. I'm never leaving you, and I know that you will never leave me. My heart beats for your presence.

James 1:1 (TPT) – *"...I'm a love-slave of God and of the Lord Jesus Christ..."*

DAY 36

J esus, I set my eyes on you today. I put all my faith in you. I believe you. I believe what you say. I believe your word. You are the word. Everything about you is true, for you are truth. Your character is truth. I look to the unseen realm even when the seen realm looks impossible. I believe what you say about me. I place all my trust and all my faith in you. Help me to follow through with my faith by action. Belief alone will not advance me. I want to be like Abraham and exchange my faith for your righteousness. I want right-standing before you. I am committed to doing and acting on what I say I believe. I fully attach myself to living it out before you. I will love you by doing what I say I believe.

When you instruct me, and it looks impossible, I will obey you and act on your instruction. When your word says that I receive promises, I will act on that word and live as if I have the promises because your word says I have them already by faith. I want to please you. I want to obey you. See me as your righteousness. See me as one so in love with you. May my life in its fullness be a living act of love to you. I honor you with my faith. I want to bring you joy with the actions of my life. I want to love you with my whole heart. Exchange all of this and accept it as my love for you.

James 2:23 - 24 (TPT) — *"So in this way, the Scripture was fulfilled: Because Abraham believed God, his faith was exchanged for God's righteousness. So he became known as the lover of God! So now it's clear that a person is seen as righteous in God's eyes not merely by faith alone, but by his works."*

DAY 37

J esus, it is so wonderful to be with you today. I have enjoyed every moment. Thank you that you are my shield. You protect me because you love me. You protect me because I am yours. I belong to you. I love how you surround me. Your presence is a field of protection around me. Nothing can penetrate your presence. You not only shield me on one side, but you are a shield around me on all sides. There is no place left unprotected because that's just how wonderful you are. You amaze me even in your beauty of protecting and shielding me. You take me into yourself and protect me. You are all around me surrounding me. To know you in this way only deepens my love for you. I feel so secure in knowing love himself protects me in the fullest, most intimate way. Let me stay in this place of safety with you, my Shield and Lover of my soul.

Psalm 3:3 (TPT) – "But in the depths of my heart I truly know that you, Yahweh, have become my Shield; You take me and surround me with yourself. Your glory covers me continually…"

A Passion Translation Footnote – "Many translations render this 'You are a shield around me.' The ancient Hebrew can be translated, 'You, O Lord, are my taker' (Augustine). The implication is that God shields us by taking us into himself. Jesus Christ is the savior of humanity, the one who was made flesh. He not only took our nature, but he also took our sins that he might take us into glory."

Day 38

Jesus, your face is so beautiful. Your features are so lovely. You are altogether perfect. You are the one I love. I spend my waking moments thinking about you, wanting more of you, wanting to be face-to-face with you. You continually reveal more of yourself to me – filling me with more and more of you. I'm so thankful for the joy you saturate me with, the bliss you set before me, and the victorious resurrection life you purchased for me. The continual revelation of resurrection life is the path that brings me face-to-face with you. I want your presence. I want to see your face. I want to set my eyes on beauty himself, life himself, and love himself. I am forever changed by your presence. I am transformed by your face. I love you. May the love I have for you reflect the intensity and passion of my desire for you.

Psalm 16:11 (TPT) – *"For you bring me a continual revelation of resurrection life, the path to the bliss that brings me face-to-face with you."*

A Passion Translation Footnote – "There is no Hebrew word for *'presence.'* When the Psalmist wanted to speak of God's presence, he used the Hebrew word for *'face.'*"

DAY 39

Jesus, how can I tell you the depth of my love for you? As I love you, you reveal layer upon layer of depth I could only imagine. My mind can only contemplate what the future layers hold. I obey your instruction to seek your face. I desire to obey you completely and fully. I need your help to succeed. The innermost part of my being needs you, wants you, and desperately seeks your face. How beautiful you are to me. You are light to my soul. You are a sweet fragrance to me. You are the total of all I need and desire. It is you alone, nothing else. My direction is always toward you. My focus is on your face. My gaze is fixed. My commitment is unwavering. My decision is settled. It is you I want. I seek you in the morning, in the evening, and in the night. I know that I have found you. I know you are mine. I will never stop leaning into you, chasing you, and seeking you with everything I am. Be so happy, Jesus, with my love for you.

Psalm 27:8 (TPT) – "Lord, when you said to me, 'Seek my face,' my inner being responded, 'I'm seeking your face with all my heart.'"

DAY 40

I crave every moment of being with you, Jesus. Above everything in my life, I want you. I desire to live with you, not apart from you. I want to be so close to you in the secret place you have just for me. I want to be so near to you that I am not only in your presence but fully seeing your face. I want to touch you. I want to see the features of your face. I want to look in your eyes. I want to see love looking at me. I want to see the one – You – that fills all my dry places with pure loveliness. I am filled with awe living with you in your house, in the bliss you have created for me to enjoy. I delight in your glory. I am covered by the weightiness of your presence. Your grace sustains me and enables me. Take pleasure in my prayers to you, in the words I speak to you, in my communing with you. Take joy in how I live my life for you. You did it all for me. Now, I do it all for you.

Psalm 27:4 (TPT) – *"Here's the one thing I crave from God, the one thing I seek above all else: I want the privilege of living with him every moment in his house, finding the sweet loveliness of his face, filled with awe, delighting in his glory and grace. I want to live my life so close to him that he takes pleasure in my every prayer."*

Day 41

Jesus, you are so good to me. I am so thankful that you love me. I love how you see me. My heart is so full of you. The way you look at me is unlike any other. Your love for me surpasses all. Your grace for me is perfect; your forgiveness, unmatchable. Your mercy and compassion for me are absolute. You love and care for me in a way no one else can. You have eyes of pure love for me. You are love himself looking at me. Your eyes and gaze are always on me. Your thoughts are always toward me. You see me as the one you love. You have given yourself for me totally and completely. Your gaze radiates into my soul. Every moment you are positioned toward me. Help me love you the way you love me. You are so good to me. Your love never ends, never runs out, never diminishes, and never changes. Help me to comprehend and be saturated in your amazing and incomprehensible love that is all for me. I am in awe that as I look to you, you are always looking at me through the eyes of perfect love.

Psalm 25:6-7 (TPT) – *"…Always look at me through your eyes of love – your forgiving eyes of mercy and compassion. When you think of me, see me as the one you love and care for. How good you are to me!"*

DAY 42

Jesus, I love you. I love everything about you. I love that you are everything I need and everything I can even desire. You fulfill every longing I have, every craving, and every lack. You give me everything I need. You give me the desires of my heart. You help me make my ways your ways. You help me to exchange my thoughts for your thoughts. You know just the right time for everything. Your ways are above my ways. As I grow, I am changed into your likeness, and your ways become mine. I wrap my heart into yours. Mold me into you. Shape me and transform me.

I wait on you. I want to be with you, to be in your presence. I want to see your face. I want your heart. I want my life to reflect the beauty of us becoming so tightly wrapped together that we are inseparable. There is just us together. My waiting is simply being with you, and, in being with you, being intertwined where there is no boundary between us. The veil has been lifted. The barrier has been broken. We are one in heart and purpose – wrapped in the beauty of being together.

Psalm 25:5 (TPT) – "*...I have wrapped my heart into yours!*"

A Passion Translation Footnote – "The Hebrew word most commonly translated as 'wait' (wait upon the Lord) is '*qavah*,' which also means 'to tie together by twisting' or 'to entwine' or 'to wrap tightly.' This is a beautiful concept of waiting upon God, not as something passive, but entwining our hearts with him and his purposes."

DAY 43

There is only one who can satisfy me, who can fill me, who can complete me. It is you, my beloved, Jesus. Jesus, you are the one I love, and you are mine. I love you in the depths of my being. I adore you with all that is within me. There is no one else like you, Jesus. I am struck by your beauty. I am transformed by your grace. I am taken with your love. I desire to stay in the secluded secret place for all of eternity just loving you alone. I have not been deceived by immature infatuation. I have been consumed by a fire of intense love that is only matched and surpassed by your love for me. To comprehend your love for me is immeasurable and indescribable. Reveal to me layer upon sweet layer of love so true and divine that my life can be devoted to returning the same perfect love to you. You are so pure and lovely and true. You are the only one worthy of being loved as my one and only beloved.

Song of Songs 5:10 (TPT) – *"He alone is my beloved…"*

DAY 44

Jesus, I am loving you at this moment. I will continue to love you for all the moments of my life. You show your love to me with the sweetest of kisses. They are filled with whispers of your passionate, consuming love for me. You are so perfect. Everything about you is so perfect. There is no flaw or imperfection about you. You are pristine. You are exquisite from every perspective. You are the perfect one I seek. I love you with a love that grows and deepens day by day, moment by moment. I love you because you are you. You loved me first, but now I love you in return. There is no one like you. You are my completer; you are my confidant; you are my friend forever. There is nowhere I would rather be than with you and being loved by you. You fill my soul with delight. It is pure. It is holy. I want my love for you to reflect your love for me.

Song of Songs 5:16 (TPT) – *"Most sweet are his kisses, even his whispers of love. He is delightful in every way and perfect from every viewpoint. If you ask me why I love him so, O brides-to-be, it's because there is none like him to me. Everything about him fills me with holy desire! Now he is my beloved – my friend, forever."*

DAY 45

Jesus, you have come to my rescue again. You constantly show me mercy and grace and love. When my feelings and emotions want to dominate, you step in close to me and gently remind me of your love for me and that I can "let you" be my everything. You smother me with divine love. I want to enter the doorway of your heart. I yield my heart and surrender all of myself to you because you are more than enough for me. There is nothing I can do but "let you." Help me to stop doing and just yield, to give way to you. I let down my arms in surrender and open them to you. I raise the white flag to my own ability and relinquish all of myself to you. I yield my own limited power to your supreme victorious power. Jesus, I "let you" into me. Take me and use me, love me and keep me.

Song of Songs 1:2 (TPT) – *"Let him smother me with kisses – his Spirit-kiss divine…"*

A Passion Translation Footnote – "To enter the doorway of Jesus' heart, we must begin by saying, 'Let him.' We only bring him a yielded heart and must 'let him' do the rest. God's loving grace means that he will be enough for us. We can 'let him' be everything to us. We don't begin by doing but by yielding."

Day 46

Jesus, I love you. You are truly the only one who can love me as you do. It is because of your suffering that perfect love can be mine. I cannot imagine fully what you felt, what excruciating agony you endured, and what forsakenness you questioned. Jesus, help me to understand this kind of love. You sweated drops of blood in anticipation of this suffering. You are fully God and fully human, but never once chose wrong. Even when you could have chosen to end the torture and pain, you endured because you were looking at me – your joy.

You took every evil, painful, sinful thing upon yourself and because of love, you endured and were victorious. You are like a tied-up bundle of myrrh resting over my heart. You were nailed to the cross and hung there in shame and humiliation, taking the worst of the worst for me. You even defeated death. You conquered all of hell for me, and you walked through fire for me. Love did not want me to endure shame and suffering. You – Love – did it for me. You will be over my heart all my days. You will be living in my heart. You will be my heart.

Song of Songs 1:13 (TPT) – *"A sachet of myrrh is my lover, like a tied-up bundle of myrrh resting over my heart."*

A Passion Translation Footnote – "This bundle of tied-up myrrh is an incredible picture of the cross. Myrrh, known as an embalming spice, is always associated with suffering. The suffering love of Jesus will be over her heart for the rest of her days – the revelation of our Beloved tied onto the cross like a bundle of myrrh."

DAY 47

Jesus, how I love you more and more, deeper and deeper every day. You have come into me so lovingly, and I have given you all of myself. There is a vineyard of love where we meet where seeds have been planted. The vineyard is yielding the beautiful fruit of our love. I will keep this beautiful place protected. I do not want any hindrances to our relationship. I will not let a sly little fox come in to raid our garden. My heart is guarded, and I will search out hidden trespassers. I want my "yes" to be "yes," and my "no" to be "no." I do not want any compromises that are hiding in secret to snatch the fruit harvest we will reap. I love you with a fierceness, and I pledge to remove any hindrance to our oneness and fullness together. Our relationship is true and pure. Our unity is untainted. In our vineyard is where love abides and grows. You and I will guard and protect our beautiful secret place together.

Song of Songs 2:15 (TPT) – *"You must catch the troubling foxes, those sly little foxes that hinder our relationship. For they raid our budding vineyard of love to ruin what I've planted within you. Will you catch them and remove them for me? We will do it together.*

A Passion Translation Footnote – "These 'foxes' are the compromises that are hidden deep in our hearts. These are areas of our lives where we have not yet allowed the victory of Christ to shine into. The foxes keep the fruit of his Spirit from growing within us."

DAY 48

Jesus, I sing to you of my overwhelming love. The melody rising out of my soul conveys my highest praise to you and my deepest yearning for you. I can see this melody streaming out of the hidden secret place, and it is flowing upward in soft majestic circles, billowing as it ascends to you. The visual representation is likened to incense, a beautiful aroma that is pleasing to you. I wanted to be the composer of this melody, but it was co-written by the Holy Spirit, and I am offering it to you as part of my acts of love.

It is a representation and manifestation of all that I long for in being with you, how I adore you, how I love you with every fiber of my being. This musical gift to you has words that I haven't yet heard, but I know they are the desire of my heart. It is a song that began when you created me, and it has no end. For ages to come, I will still be playing this beautiful composition which has your justice, your love, your grace, and your absolute perfection as its theme. May my life bring forth and show so clearly my love and adoration for you, through this never-ending melody played by the orchestra of my heart.

Psalm 101:1 (TPT) – *"Lord, I will sing about your faithful love for me. My song of praise will have your justice as its theme."*

DAY 49

I am swept away when I imagine the elders worshiping you in Heaven. When I contemplate the scene of you at the center of everything and receiving praise and worship and love and adoration, my heart is overcome with emotion. I can't help but long for this day. How glorious to be in your presence along with the mass congregation of worshippers all joining in to proclaim how worthy you are. I love you more than anything or anyone. You are the only one worthy of my praise. There is no one else worthy. Let it be on earth as it is in heaven.

So, I worship you now without ceasing, day and night. I sing to you "Holy, holy, holy are you!" You are the Almighty! You are within me, and you never change. As you were yesterday, you are today, and you will be tomorrow. You are the coming one. Be everything to me as you always have been and are now and will always be. How can I fully express my desire to be with you? See the intensity in my heart for you. I continually cast all I have at your feet and worship and sing to you. You are the only one for me.

Revelation 4:8 (TPT) – "...*They worshiped without ceasing, day and night, singing, 'Holy, holy, holy is the Lord God, the Almighty! The Was, the Is, and the Coming!'*"

Passion Translation Footnotes – "He who was (Christ) in his early life is now the one who is within us."

"Or 'the coming one.' He is coming to be all that he is within us."

DAY 50

J esus, I love you today more than ever. I commit myself to loving you all of my days. I don't just want to love you, but I want my love for you to be the best I have to give you. I know that I am yours and will always be yours and you will never stop loving me. You tell me that I am your darling, the one you think about day and night. I cannot stray from having you above all else. Even though I have made a settled decision to keep you foremost, my heart will not let me drift away from loving you.

I have come too far with you to stray now. My love for you is passionate and rises high above any other thing or person that would try to be the object of my affection. I want to love you so well and so perfectly that you will be pleased. I want your jealousy for me. I want to be desirable to you. I want to be the one you desire to be with forever. No, I will never abandon or forget my first love, the love that kindled my heart, the love that was fanned by the wind of absolute purity and truth, the love that is now a raging fire that cannot be contained.

Revelation 2:4 (TPT) – *"But I have this against you: you have abandoned the passionate love you had for me at the beginning."*

Passion Translation Footnotes – "The meaning of Ephesus is 'desirable' or 'darling.' Every church and every believer are desirable to Jesus Christ, for we are his bride. This is the word a Greek bridegroom would use for the girl he desired to marry…"

"Or 'you have abandoned your first love.' The Greek word for *first* (protos) means 'foremost,' 'best,' 'paramount,' 'supreme,' 'crowning,' 'number one.' Jesus is referring to exclusive love that has first place in our hearts above all else."

DAY 51

Jesus, I am fixed on you. I raise my eyes toward you. You are where I want to be. I close my eyes to the past. There is no room for me there. I do not remember what I have left behind to pursue you, as I have no worthy opportunity in the past. I am desperately longing for you. I am yearning for the heavenly city where we will dwell with each other. My eyes of faith are open. My heart is looking ahead. There is something far greater than where I have been. Open the gates of the heavenly realm for me so that I may enter and be in your presence. I live in expectation of you. My life, in its sum, is only to be with you. I love everything about you. Until the physical city appears, let this heavenly city be established in my heart. There I will dwell with you and be with you, drinking in your presence, beholding your lovely face, and gazing into your eyes of love.

Hebrews 11:14-16 (TPT) — *"For clearly, those who live this way are longing for the appearing of a heavenly city! If their hearts were still remembering what they left behind, they would have found an opportunity to go back. However, they couldn't turn back for their hearts were fixed on what was far greater, that is, the heavenly realm!"*

DAY 52

Jesus be unveiled to me. Let me have a greater revelation of you. Remove the barrier between us so that I can see your face clearly. I want to see who you are, your nature, the essence of you. Let me know you by all your names. Let me know all your attributes. Give me knowledge of you, but, even more, give me yourself. I want to be with you. I want to live with you. I want to step into you and receive the fullness of you. I want to dine with you and have continual communion with you. I want your blood and your body.

I take all of you for all of me. I want to be one with you in all your glory. I want to see you for who you really are. Take away my own preconceived ideas of you. Remove from me what I have heard about you. I want you to reveal yourself to me, just you and me. Speak to me directly. Just be with me. I want to know you for myself because I need you. I'm searching for you, and I'm knocking at the door of your heart. Lift the veil and let me in. Thank you that it is your desire to be unveiled to me even more than my desire to make you known to me. I love you.

Colossians 3:4 (TPT) – *"And as Christ himself is seen for who he really is, who you really are will also be revealed, for you are now one with him in his glory!"*

DAY 53

J esus, I have a longing to dwell with you. I am a stranger here. I
am in a foreign land. My body is here, but my soul and spirit are
restless. My soul goes from place to place with a need to settle,
but there is no place worthy or acceptable. Let me transcend this
earthly realm into the heavenly realm to be with you. I need comfort
and stability. I need you. The place I am yearning for is the secret
place with you. I love being in the shadow of your wings. Just as
Adam walked with you and you spoke to him in the cool of the day,
I want that to be my experience. I want that to be my life. I want my
life to be lived right next to you, to be pulled into you.

Cover me with yourself, cover me with the wings of protection.
Circle around me and give me a habitation of rest, of love, of just
being with you. I do not belong anywhere but with you. I am a
stranger in a foreign land looking toward you. You are my
destination, my journey, and my roadmap. You are all things to me,
Jesus. I feel like my soul and spirit could leap out of my body to get
to you. Thank you that on my quest to be with you, you have
overwhelmed me and already chased me down. You have met me
and brought yourself to me. You have provided me the secret place
right where I am because you love me. I am so in love with you Jesus.

Hebrews 11:13 (TPT) – *"…They all lived their lives on earth as those
who belonged to another realm."*

A Passion Translation Footnote – "Or 'as strangers and nomads
on earth.'"

DAY 54

Jesus, how I love you. How I long for you. My heart is churning like a violent raging sea with a desire to reach the shores of life with you. There is no stopping until the waves of my soul reach you. My heart beats at a rate so fast I feel like it may pound out of my chest. See my yearning for you. See my desire to please you. See my willingness to obey. Work wonders in my life, Jesus. I am devoted to you. I am your lover. Hear my prayers. Hear my requests. Hear the desperate panting of my pleas. I know that you will never leave me. I know that you will never turn your eyes from me. You have wonderful things for me. You love me with an unrelenting fierceness that dissipates all fear.

Take away my trembling. I only sit in your presence with your peace flooding over my soul. Release me from the demands of those who do not hear your voice. I don't see the escape, but I do see you. Thank you that you are my escape. You are my refuge from the storm. Take me into you and shield me from torment. Take me and reveal to me your marvelous love. Set me apart for you. As the winds try to toss me from place to place with no restful, loving habitation, you gently and lovingly pull me into you and answer my prayer. I will never forget the wonderful things you do for me. Hear me tell you how much I love you.

Psalm 4:3 (TPT) – *"May we never forget that the Lord works wonders for every one of his devoted lovers. This is how I know that he will answer my every prayer."*

A Passion Translation Footnote – "…Some manuscripts read 'The Lord sets apart a faithful one for himself.' Another possible translation is 'The Lord has revealed to me his marvelous love.'"

Day 55

Jesus, I am here again today to love you. You have provoked my heart, and I am confident it will burst from the volume of love that has accumulated. I ask you to enlarge me. Enlarge my capacity to love you. Enlarge my desire for you. There is nothing I am not willing to lay before you. I give you my life, my breath, and my children. I give you all the pieces of my life including my career, my house, and my vehicles. I give you all my finances. I give you back all my talents and gifts. Jesus, I don't want any of these things without you. Let me lie in an open forest with no covering if I don't have you. Take all these things – all the pieces of my life – and shape them and polish them. Remove them if necessary.

I only want what your perfect plan is for me. That can only come from you. Clean and purify me. Let your fire fall on all of me and burn away the dead parts. Prune branches of my life that drain me and are unproductive. Help me to see your plan amid the cleansing. Your ways are so much higher than my ways, and I fully trust you. I tell you every day that I love you. Those are not just words I speak to you. Know that those words coupled with my life given to you represent the richness of my very essence and all I have to offer you. I say yes to you. I am yours like a chess piece. Move me where you want me. Position me where you will. I am here for you. Take me and use me. Love me and preserve me. I give it all to you.

Psalm 5:3 (TPT) – *"...Every morning I lay out the pieces of my life on the altar and wait for your fire to fall upon my heart."*

Day 56

Jesus, I am so glad that you are mine. I have everything that is yours. Today is the dawning of a new era. I will love your word, each letter, syllable, and definition. I will take your name and love it and cherish it. Your name is so priceless and valuable. I have your name as my own. I am in such awe that I can use your name with authority, and it is backed by all of heaven. Your name is sweeter than any other name. It is higher than any other name. When I think about the majesty of your name, I bow. Jesus. How sweet and pure and holy.

There are hidden mysteries in your name. Draw me to you and reveal more to me. I am so full of joy to dwell in your presence. Overshadow me. The bubbling inside me is a fountain which is shouting of my joy because of you. As I whisper your beautiful name, I hold it so tightly to my heart. As I speak forth your name boldly, I speak authority and dominion. As I shout your name, I send for gladness and joy in the heavens and the earth. How much I love your name. I speak it over and over – out loud and in my heart. I love you. Jesus.

Psalm 5:11 (TPT) – *"But let them all be glad, those who turn aside to hide themselves in you. May they keep shouting for joy forever! Overshadow them in your presence as they sing and rejoice. Then every lover of your name will burst forth with endless joy."*

Day 57

Jesus, I am so thankful for you. I love you with all of myself. I wish I had other words to express my desire for you. You have done everything for me. You have finished it all. Your work is finished. Completed. There is nothing left for me to do. I love how you are now. You are the victorious one. You are the conqueror. You now have the keys to death. You are above all things. You are *The Most High*. There is nothing and no one higher. Your name is above every name. You sit at the right hand of God right now. You are so glorious and lovely and beautiful. You are all mine. You have made me to be like you – just as you are now. Thank you that because of you, I am victorious and can conquer all things. Thank you that because I have your name, I have the power and authority of your name right now.

You are like no other. Not only do you give your love to me, but you provide the good life for me. Even though darts are fired in my direction and I may go through life's deepest challenges, I get through them because of you. I not only get through, but you make me the head and not the tail. You are grace himself. You make me pure and holy, seated with you on the right side of God. Thank you that I have right standing before God. When he looks at me, all he sees is you. Thank you for standing up for me and loving me. Your love is so perfect and so pure. It is absolute love. You are love. From you flows all good and wonderful things. I am continually falling deeper and deeper in love with you. I want to be just like you. The more time I spend with you, the more I am transformed. Just like when God looks at me, when I look at myself, all I want to see is you.

1 John 4:17 (TPT) – *"…because all that Jesus now is, so are we in this world."*

A Passion Translation Footnote – "Or 'because we are what he is in this world.' The verb tense is important. We are not like Jesus was, but because of grace, we are like he is now: pure and holy, seated in heaven, and glorified… Faith has transferred his righteousness to us."

DAY 58

Jesus, I desire to walk with you today. Take my hand and walk through the beautiful garden of our love today. I want to be with you in paradise. Just you and me together. I need time with you. Let's go on a quiet, peaceful stroll as we enjoy the beautiful flowers and trees while talking to each other. Come, and you pick the place. Let's stay there all day and be together. Breathe your breath over me. It is life to my spirit. There is a beautiful mystery to this scene of our garden paradise. Your light has shone on me, your bride, the one you love. It is me, where you now find paradise. I am your beautiful one, your sanctuary, your paradise garden. Your mysteries are wonderful and colored with beauty. The mystery here is like a mirror reflecting us onto each other. I see you, and you see me as the desire and ultimate love for each other – bringing back the original design of creation for your perfect love.

Song of Songs 4:16 (TPT) – "...*Come walk with me as you walked with Adam in your paradise garden...*"

A Passion Translation Footnote – "The scene of a garden and the breath of God point us back to Eden. Now, this paradise is found in his bride. This is the reason the reference of Adam is given: to help the reader connect with the mystery of this scene..."

DAY 59

Jesus, you have always been and will always be. You have no beginning or end. You are eternal. You have always been for me and will always be with me. Your love for me is eternal. You are the highest in all of creation. You are the Creator. You are God in the flesh. You are the Word. You are every letter, every combination of letters, the very sum of all language. Because you are the eternal Word, you brought forth creation by your self-expression. You are the very presence of God that I long for. Your self-expression is so creative, so unique, and yet so orderly. Everything that exists is because of you. Jesus, you are the Message. Any other message is beneath you. You are the focus. You are the Blueprint. You are the master plan. You are perfection in visible form.

You are so much bigger and all-encompassing that I cannot fully comprehend, yet you are the one I long for every moment. I exist just to be tucked away next to you and enjoy your presence, your closeness, and your loveliness. Whenever I have needed you, you were there. You have always been. As I need you now, you are here. On my journey in this life, I know you will always be with me. You never end. You are everywhere at once. You are in the past, present, and future all at once. You transcend all of time. You amaze me. I'm so much in awe of you and every facet of your being. Let me know you more. Let me understand you more. Let me be with you and love you always in a way that comes close to how you love me. My desire is to love you eternally. Can my love travel back to reach you where it has no beginning? Help me to love you so absolutely and with such purity now. Let my love for you go forward to reach you and surround your heart for all eternity with no end.

John 1:1 (TPT) – *"In the very beginning the Living Expression was already there."*

A Passion Translation Footnote – "The Greek is logos, which has a rich and varied background in both Greek philosophy and Judaism. The Greeks equated logos with the highest principle of cosmic order. God's logos in the Old Testament is his powerful self-expression in creation, revelation, and redemption. In the New Testament, we have this new unique view of God given to us by John, which signifies the presence of God himself in the flesh. Some have translated this rich term as "Word." It could also be translated as "Message" or "Blueprint." Jesus Christ is the eternal Word, the creative Word, and the Word made visible. He is the divine self-expression of all that God is, contains, and reveals in incarnated flesh. Just as we express ourselves in words, God has perfectly expressed himself in Christ."

DAY 60

Jesus, as I meditate on everything about you, I travel deeper and deeper into a place of love for you. I marvel at your hand, at your power. I sit at your feet in awe of you. I am nothing without you. Truly, nothing at all. I would not exist without you. You thought of me in your creative inspiration and through your power created me. You wanted to love me. You designed me and formed me. You gave yourself for me because of your love for me. Help me to never forget how special I am to you. I am not insignificant to you. I am the apple of your eye. You held me and blew your breath into me and gave me life. You have not only given me an existence; you have given me true life. You gave me a natural, physical life that is so wonderful. You have also given me spiritual, eternal, never-ending life!

None of this could have happened apart from you. I am powerless on my own. Even though I may try or have perseverance, I am still absolutely nothing without you. I have no life without you. I merely exist without you, wobbling and ready to fall into the pit of darkness forever. I love you, Jesus. You had love in mind before you created me. Love was always; Love is always; Love will always be because you are Love. Because you are Love, you created me. You wanted to give yourself to me. You wanted me to have Love for myself. How can I convey just how much I return your love? Everything is in your hand, your power. Now I give myself to you. I love you with all my might and with all my power. I love you with all the creative inspiration you have put into me. I love you with all my life, with all of my breath. I love you because you are Love. I love you because you loved me first. I love you because you are you.

John 1:3-4 (TPT) – *"And through his creative inspiration this Living Expression made all things, for nothing has existence apart from him! Life came into being because of him, for his life is light for all humanity."*

A Passion Translation Footnote – "Or 'all things happened because of him, and nothing happened apart from him.' The Aramaic is, 'everything was in his hand' (of power) …"

Day 61

Jesus, you are absolute loveliness and beauty. You cannot be less than this. As the creative genius that imagined the universe and every detail thereof, your character is so evident in your work. When I look at the splendor and glorious nature of the work of your hands, it all points back to you, the creator. The moon and the stars are a masterpiece on the canvas of the universe you have prepared for my enjoyment. They are like exquisite jewels adorning the sky.

You are my love, my everything. It is you I praise for the wonderful artistic creation that exists. I know that just as the moon and the stars were created and placed so perfectly, you have created me and placed me just where you want me. Thank you that I am made beautiful in your sight. You are the most beautiful thing before my eyes. You encompass my vision. You, who are everything to me, my creator, the one I love, are gazing at me, your creation, with your eyes of love for me. I adore you. I love you. Create in me a deeper need, a deeper desire, and a deeper capacity to love you — creator and lover of my soul – Jesus.

Psalm 8:3 (TPT) – *"Look at the splendor of your skies, your creative genius glowing in the heavens. When I gaze at your moon and your stars, mounted like jewels in their settings, I know you are the fascinating artist who fashioned it all!"*

Day 62

Jesus, you are fully divine, yet you are fully human. You are fully God and fully man – in your earthly state and your eternal state. I marvel at you. I love you. You came to earth to experience humanity, with the purpose of achieving total victory for me. A star appeared to guide the wise men to you. They looked to the heavens for direction and found you. I look to the heavens for you also. When you came, you outshined all other stars. Your light shone more purely and more absolutely than all other lights. You are the bright Morning Star. You call yourself the bright Morning Star, so I call you the bright Morning Star.

You are the one I look to. Your light shines with love for me, and I follow it. Your light is truth. Your light is love. Shine on me and in me. Illuminate my soul with your love and goodness. My life bends toward you like a flower, following the sunlight throughout the day, receiving energy, love, and life. I lean into you. I posture myself in your direction. Because you are so close to me, I do this with ease, and it satisfies all my need for your touch. Reflect off me. When others see me, let them see your light reflecting on me. Let them see that you are mine and I am yours. I love you. I need you. I want you. I must have you. You are my everything…my bright Morning Star.

Revelation 22:16 (TPT) – "*…I am the bright Morning Star….*"

DAY 63

I love you, Jesus! I bless you today. Let your name be on my lips continually. Let my love extend to you in the wonderful times and in challenging times. I worship you, Jesus. You are the one I love, the one I long for. You have told me that you love me. You continually show your love to me. Your love is everlasting. It cannot run out, and it will never end. It lasts forever. It is eternal just as you are eternal. You are Love, so Love can never end. You are unchanging, the same in the past, the present, and the future. What you have spoken to me cannot change. Thank you for never changing. Thank you that you cannot change.

Thank you that Love never changes toward me. It always has me at the center of your focus, at the center of your heart.

Such a wonderful and merciful love is this that it would follow me and constantly remind me of your presence. Even when I don't feel Love, you are with me, drawing me to yourself, closer and closer. Your desire is even stronger than mine for us to be dwelling in the same habitation. Mold my desires into your desires. Let my wishes be your wishes. Let our hearts' desires be one, matching and complementing at the same time. Your love is unfailing. It never lets me down. It is perfect in all its ways. You are Love; you are unfailing, you are Everlasting Love drawing me toward you. I love you, Jesus. Draw me closer. Love me, unrelentingly.

Jeremiah 31:3 (NLT) – "... *I have loved you, my people, with an everlasting love. With unfailing love, I have drawn you to myself.*'"

Day 64

I love you, Jesus. Thank you that the veil between us has been lifted. Thank you that there is no separation and no barrier between us. I don't want a dim and obstructed view of you. I want to see you clearly and know you fully. Let nothing separate us. More than transparency; let there be a joining of us in spirit so that there is no separation at all. Lift the barrier. Let there be no veil between us, no hiding from each other, and no covering to separate us. I look at you, the one I love, and say, "Here you are!" You are mine. I am yours. You are so worthy of being the only one I love. I love you above and beyond any other. The words I use are not adequate to describe your insurmountable position. None can surpass you. Some will try to get beyond your summit, but none will achieve it. I have chosen you. You alone. Be with me so close. I look to you in awe, in adoration, in love as you lift the veil. I am enveloped in your glory, completely undone, and ravished in the most passionate way by who you are.

Revelation 1:1 (TPT) – *"This is the unveiling of Jesus Christ..."*

A Passion Translation Footnote – "The Greek noun *"apokalypsis"* is a compound word found eighteen times in the New Testament. It combines apo (to lift) with *kaluptó* (veil, hide, cover), and so could be translated 'the lifting of the veil' or 'the unveiling.' The implication could be stated as simply, 'Here he is!' It is not primarily lifting the veil off coming events, but the unveiling of Jesus."

DAY 65

Jesus, thank you for loving me. You orchestrated such a wonderful plan of restoration for me. What you created for me to enjoy is not lost. The paradise that you created which was tainted by sin is no longer removed from me. You created a wonderful place for me to dwell - a paradise garden for me to enjoy the land, the vegetation, the beauty of the landscape, and a place to dwell with you. This is a place where we commune. It is where we walk every day and talk and share of ourselves. You created a wonderful Tree of Life in this paradise for me. You want me to feast on the fruit of the Tree of Life, to enjoy all its benefits.

The beauty of what you restore is that I now have access to all this wonderful creation and design that was intended for me. This paradise is now in my heart. I love you, and you dwell in me. You are in my heart. You are the hope of glory, and you are now in my heart. We dwell together in the secret place. I have pulled you into me, and there is life-giving fruit of our relationship that I will enjoy — what an excellent plan. You are the God of wonder. You are the God of everything that is good. You are good. You are love. What was lost to me forever is now dwelling in my very heart. Thank you, Jesus, that you desire to live in me. Let my heart be a beautiful and pure dwelling place for you to inhabit. Take up residence and dwell in me forever. I love you, Jesus.

Revelation 2:7 (TPT) – "...*To the one who overcomes I will give access to feast on the fruit of the Tree of Life that is found in the paradise of God.*"

A Passion Translation Footnote – "The paradise of God is now found within the hearts of Jesus' loving followers… The Tree of Life is Christ within us, the hope of glory. The fruit of that tree is reserved for those who overcome."

Day 66

Jesus, I love you. I love your words. I love everything you say to me. I cherish all your words. I cling to every word you speak. I want my words to be your words. Let my lips be obedient and submit to what is in my heart. You are in my heart, Jesus. You are Love himself. You dwell in me. Let my obedience to you reflect my love for you. Let my words be generated from the Love that dwells inside me. Let my words be like a honeycomb to you, like milk and honey, sweet and satisfying to your ears. Transform me into your likeness, into your image, into a reflection of Love. Let only You flow from me. Let only You fill the container of my life.

Fill me so full that everything else is pushed out. Consume me so fully that I have no room left for second best. I want You alone. You are the only one so perfect and so complete that satisfies me – for I crave your milk and honey. Fill me with all of you, so the only thing flowing from me is your milk and honey. At this juncture, I will become the Promised Land for you as an eternal dwelling place. This is my desire. I want to be your desire. I don't want to be a developing and immature Promised Land that is not yet inhabited, but a fully developed and mature Promised Land – one you have invaded and possessed and one where you have established to dwell eternally.

Song of Songs 4:11 (TPT) – *"Your loving words are like the honeycomb to me; your tongue releases milk and honey, for I find the Promised Land flowing within you."*

A Passion Translation Footnote – "Both the Promised Land and your heart flow with milk and honey. You have become the Promised Land of Jesus Christ."

Day 67

Jesus, I love you. Let my life flow into yours. Let purity be seen as this garden spring flows. There isn't a quantifiable amount of water inside me, but, instead, there is a well of living water springing up. I am like a mountain brook that started somewhere small but has grown and matured. This brook has turned into a stream and has continued to wind and flow over the terrain of my soul. It became a flowing river that has approached the falls. As the crystal-clear water approaches and cascades over the falls, it turns into a majestic and powerful representation of the life source within me.

This never-ending life source within me is you, Jesus. My spring would dry, and my terrain would be barren without you. Now there is beauty and life flowing from my deep inward well. See yourself flowing from my life. See the majestic waterfall and smile. See the mist and the sun shining through beautiful rainbow prisms, which remind me of how wonderful your promises are to me. We are united as one. As your life becomes my deep well of living water, the cascading falls flow back to you. The nature of our love and unity is beautiful. Be my never-ending source, and I will eternally flow back to you, my destination, my habitation, my dwelling place.

Song of Songs 4:15 (TPT) – *"Your life flows into mine, pure as a garden spring. A well of living water springs up from within you, like a mountain brook flowing into my heart."*

DAY 68

Jesus, you are the love of my life. You are the originator and creator of my life. Your creativity designed me. I was designed to be loved by you and to love you. I was designed to be your bride. You are more precious to me than anything. You are far greater than diamonds and pearls. You are more valuable than land and real estate. You are the most valuable, and you are priceless. You paid the ultimate price for me. You bought me back from the pit. Your love for me transformed my history, my present, and my future. You, who IS perfect, gave yourself for me. You were perfected by fire when you were already perfect.

You conquered everything that opposed you, that was against you. You rose up victorious so that you could have me for yourself. You walked through fire for me. There are no impurities attached to you. There never will be. You are gold to me. You are the worthiest One. You are the truest wealth. Everything I need and desire is in you. You shine brilliantly. Your luster exceeds all others, and your value is priceless. With you, I am wealthy beyond compare. I have my heart's desire. I have my all in all, my everything. You are truly the gold standard, and nothing can surpass you. I love not just a part of you, but all of you. Thank you for being my everything. Thank you for being my true wealth. Thank you for loving me.

Revelation 3:18 (TPT) – *"So I counsel you to purchase gold perfected by fire so that you can be truly rich…"*

A Passion Translation Footnote – "That is, Christ will be our gold. The wealth of Christ is not purchased with money but by faith…"

DAY 69

Jesus, how I love you! You are constantly with me. Everywhere I go, everything I do, you are with me. I open my eyes to see you clearly. I am awake to look for you, to watch for you. I do not want to miss you. I do not want to be sleeping, and you pass by without me knowing. I am waiting and ready for you. I am prepared. You are the one I long for. All my thoughts are of you. I think about your goodness, your love, your mercy, and your peace all day. I dream about your face. I long to look in your eyes and have your gaze pull me in. I will not be unaware of your coming. I am not just existing. I have life in me because you dwell in me. I push away deadness and instead am determined to live, being awake and alert, not living in slumber. I want clear vision, no obstructions, to see you coming, as you are in truth and perfection. I love you, Jesus. You are my whole reason for living. Apart from you, there is nothing. I experience victory because of you, being dressed in a white garment, in your presence. I live in you; I dwell in you; I love you. You are my life. You are my love. I am here with eyes wide open, longing for and loving you.

Revelation 3:1 (TPT) – *"...I know all that you do, and I know that you have a reputation for being really "alive," but you're actually dead!"*

DAY 70

Jesus, I am desperately after your heart. I yearn to know your desires and to satisfy the longings of your heart. Daily, I attend to each day's activities, but amid it all, I am drawn to you. I sit quietly alone and play my instrument for you. I sing of my love for you, of my praise for you, of my need for you. I thank you for the beautiful beauty you have given me in nature to enjoy. I thank you for the full and satisfying provision you send to me. I thank you for rescuing me from my enemies. I tell you of my day, of my challenges and triumphs, of my innermost thoughts. I share my life with you. I give my life to you. I want to know you.

As the sheep know the voice of the shepherd, I want to know your voice because I have been with you day after day. Even though my daily activities may seem insignificant, I know that in the middle of insignificance, you give me great purpose. You give me strength and power. You give me the key to your heart. You open doors for me that no one can shut; and close doors for me that no one can open. You give me the stone to throw at the giant in my way. You give me favor in royal places. Let me live in your grace, with the key to your heart. I want only to know your heart intimately as I dwell with you. I am yours, and I ask you to use me. I turn the lock and open Love's heart to join with mine. Let intimacy abound. Open doors. Closed doors. Draw me into you. Draw me into your heart.

Revelation 3:7 (TPT) – *"...for these are the solemn words of the Holy One, the true one, who has David's key, who opens doors that none can shut and who closes doors that none can open..."*

A Passion Translation Footnote – "The key of David unlocks intimacy and prayer. David was a man who lived in grace centuries before the gospel of God's grace was unveiled. In that sense, the key of David allowed him to view the future and live in the grace it would reveal."

DAY 71

Jesus, I love you and welcome you into my house today. You are the only one I am inviting. I want you to not be a visitor, but to inhabit my house and my life. Dwell not only in the four walls of my house but in all the secret places of my life. Take up so much space that there is no room for anyone or anything else. You have priority. You are my only. Just as I welcome you into my dwelling place, you reciprocate. I know that I have a standing invitation to dwell in your presence. I marvel at your love for me, in your capacity to love me, in your complete love for me, in your absolute love for me. I am covered by your covenant of mercy and love. Your covenant is not breakable, and it is eternal. How can I be the one deserving of your love?

I may never know why you love me as you do, but I am so thankful. I am so full of love for you. All my moments are for you; all my living is for you; my all is for you. Let there not be separate houses where we each visit with each other, but one marital home that we share. I want to live with you, to dwell with you, to be with you. This home we share is the secret place. In the secret place, there is everything you intended for us to share, to have, to enjoy. There, I find complete contentment under the shadow of the Almighty, full of rest and protection and love. There is no doing, just being with each other. Time is irrelevant and erased. There we are... being... enjoying... loving each other.

Psalm 5:7 (TPT) – *"But I know that you will welcome me into your house, for I am covered by your covenant of mercy and love."*

DAY 72

Jesus, I love you more every day. Yesterday, I didn't think it was possible to love you more, but today, my love has surpassed all other marks. You are so good and so true – so absolute in every good and perfect way. I let your love wash over me. You are so pure. You are so radiant. You have been purified where no purifying was needed. You have always been spotless and blameless – from before time, and you will be so after time. You are far exceeding any measure I can mark. Even when I calculate, you are incalculable. How can my mind comprehend your greatness? How can I fathom your love? I sit so still and silently, barely taking a breath, just consumed by you. You reached out to me. Your arm is not too short to grab on to me. You gave me all of yourself. You paid for me with your blood. Crimson love, pour over me and wash my robe, cleanse my life, and make me white. I take your blood in exchange for you taking mine. How merciful and how full of grace is your love! Draw me near. Pull me in. Wash me completely. Saturate me in your blood. I am marked for you. Your blood runs through my veins. My heart beats with the love of the one who gave me his all.

Revelation 7:14 (TPT) – "… *They are the ones who have washed their robes and made them white in the blood of the Lamb…*"

DAY 73

Jesus, you consume me. When my feelings and emotions slip down the slope of hopelessness and despair, you are right next to me with outstretched arms ready to pick me up and pull me back to where I should be. You know just what I'm going through. You know my thoughts. You know thoughts that are fired in my direction. Thank you that you know my heart and you know my resolve. I have told you before that it is a settled issue – my complete and total love for you. I want to walk surrendered to you. I submit myself to you. I line my ways with your ways. I line my thoughts with your thoughts.

I have the mind of the one who loves me. Your love for me is beyond any words I could use to describe it. It is so far above and beyond, so high, so deep, and so wide. Your love is extravagant. It has always been and will never end. Jesus, you surrendered your life as a sacrifice for me. Now, I surrender my life to you. Your love for me is like a sweet fragrant healing, soothing balm that makes everything new and fresh. This is an aroma of adoration that rises and fills the atmosphere. Let my love for you be the same. Let my love for you be a sweet aroma of adoration, so pleasing to you, a soothing balm for your heart. Let my love for you be extravagant – all for you, my one and only.

Ephesians 5:2 (TPT) – *"And continue to walk surrendered to the extravagant love of Christ, for he surrendered his life as a sacrifice for us. His great love for us was pleasing to God, like an aroma of adoration – a sweet healing fragrance."*

DAY 74

Jesus, I love you. I choose you. I choose you no matter what happens, no matter the circumstances. I will love you no matter what comes my way. I know that you are Love and that Love himself loves me in an extravagant way, so far above and beyond what I can ever comprehend. I will love you even if I don't understand what I am walking through. Your ways are so far above my ways. Your thoughts are so much greater than my own thoughts. Transform me into a reflection of you, in my thoughts, in my words, and my deeds. I cherish you. I adore you. I need your presence above everything. I need your presence above my family. I need your presence above what I think I want. I need your presence above my own life. I would wait for all eternity to just be in your presence. Thank you that you are here with me and that you never leave me. Thank you that you have shown yourself to me and that I know you. Thank you that I have heard your voice. I would recognize your voice anywhere. You are the one I long for. You are the one I look for. You are the one I love. I choose you again and again and again. You alone. You are my only one. I choose you. I cherish you. I need you. I love you.

Psalm 140:13 (TPT) — *"Your godly lovers will thank you no matter what happens. For they choose and cherish your presence above everything else!"*

DAY 75

Jesus, I saturate myself in your presence today. I push away my own agenda and just soak in the atmosphere of you. I sit at your feet to be near you. I want to look up and see you before me, looking at me with eyes of love. You take me into yourself and protect me. You cherish me and adore me. I have found true love. I never need to search again or wonder if another is the one. It is you I was looking for all along. You release grace to me that fills all my deepest places and overflows. Thank you for unearned mercy that you continually show me. Time after time of my shortcomings, you bend toward me and with so gentle a touch, you tell me how much you love me. When I forget in a moment, and my flesh tries to step to the forefront, you mercifully step up next to me and remind me of your never-ending love for me and who I am. You take all my worry away and replace it with a peace that I cannot completely understand. You do all of this for me. You have gone to such lengths to be able to be my one and only. You are so good to me. You are absolute, perfect, full of grace and mercy. Your love is so raw and so real to me. Your love is so genuine. At last, I have found you – true love.

2 John 3 (TPT) – *"God our Father and Jesus Christ, his Son, will release to us overflowing grace, mercy, and peace, filled with true love."*

DAY 76

Jesus, you are like no other. You are matchless; you are the only one who is worthy. You are above all others. You surpass them all. As high as the heavens are, you are still higher. How can I express my love for you? How can I express my adoration for you? How can I express my praise for you? Love's light shined into my very being – the core of me and my existence. This light illuminates my soul and makes my deep dark places shine. Brilliant light emanates from you as you beam Love into my life. You have taken me and transformed me into something pleasing to you – into your most desirable! I no longer just exist, but I have abundance and fullness – real, true life. This is only because of you. I live through you, Jesus. You have created a way for me to live. You created me, and you also created a life for me. Without you, I am nothing. I am broken, tired, and displaced. I have no home. I have no purpose. With you, I have a life that overflows. You gave me yourself. You allow me to live in you, to live in your hand of grace. You have given me all things, but the most special, the most important is matchless. It is you. It is Love.

I John 4:9 (TPT) – *"The light of God's love shined within us when he sent his matchless Son into the world so that we might live through him."*

A Passion Translation Footnote – "The Aramaic can be translated 'that we might live in his hand,' considered to be an idiom for living by his grace."

DAY 77

Jesus, I love you. I try to express myself to you and what you mean to me, but in many ways it is inadequate. I know that you know my heart, and that comforts me to know that you understand me. You have loved me with a love that has no beginning. Help me to understand this and grasp all it means. Your love is so great that it was only by and because of your love that I can be free. Even though I love you with a tremendous love, it really is not comparable to yours. Yours is so perfect, so true, and so absolute for me. I can write of your love, but I ask you to take me deeper into yourself so that I can comprehend. Expand my mind. Expand my heart. Stretch me. Mold me. Transform me into what you want, into what is pleasing to you.

Invade my life. When you look at me, I want you to be pleased. I know you will never stop loving me and your love for me will never stagger or diminish, but, even so, I desperately want to love you and love you more all the time. Take my heart. Break it open and release a flood of adoration and love for you. Create a well deep within me, so this flow never ends. You loved me with no love in return. Your love was ever full, ever perfect, and eternal. Now, I love you back. I have found you. I will never let you out of my sight. You are mine, and I am most definitely yours. This is love. It is all about you. Take my love for you and hold it tightly. It is for you and only you. You are the one I love. Today, tomorrow, and for eternity.

1 John 4:10 (TPT) – *"This is love. He loved us long before we loved him. It was his love, not ours..."*

Day 78

Jesus, I love and adore you with all I have in me. I love you with all my comprehension. I love you with all my will. I love you with all my emotions. I love you with the humanity you created as part of my being. I love you no matter what I feel. I love you despite my emotions. I love you with my smile. I love you with my tears. I love you with all my heart, soul, and every fiber of my being. I love you with every last drop of energy I have. I know I am loved by you. I am the center of your delight. I am the object of your affection. I take your love and am so content and satisfied being next to you – in your presence, with you gazing down at me with eyes so complete and full of love for me. Your love for me is so inexhaustible, so pure, so untainted that I never want to leave you. I love your love. You are love, and I love you. I love you because you first loved me, but I love you just because of who you are. You find joy in me. You smile because of me. You delight in me. I revel at knowing that you delightfully love me. I love being your delight. I love how you love me.

1 John 4:11 (TPT) – *"Delightfully loved ones..."*

DAY 79

Jesus, I love you. I love your perfect love that constantly pours over me. It purifies me. It cleanses me. It heals me. It makes me whole. It makes me full. I am in awe of you. I'm in awe of how you are so matchless, so set apart, yet so close. I'm amazed at your desire to know me and to be with me. I can't comprehend the lengths you went through in giving yourself for me. The complete agony and torture you endured was all for me. It is such an amazing concept – one I cannot grasp fully. My soul is screaming inside to understand your love for me more completely. I physically ache to search the depths of you. I want to be intimate with love's perfection. I want to know you more fully in the deep realms of your heart.

Thank you that your love drives out fear.

Thank you that when your love is present, I have fullness and peace beyond anything I can understand. Thank you that your love guides me and seals me with the mark of you. Thank you that I can end all traces of rejection by allowing your love to fill up those dry, sore, desperate areas of my life. I need you, Jesus. I am desperate for you. I can't live even a moment without you. I can't live apart from you. I never want to feel fear where there is hopelessness. I never want to experience rejection without knowing a perfect love is reaching for me. As what I think I want walks by without acknowledging me, you are still with me. In you are all my hopes and dreams, all my desires, all I can ever have or be. It is in you alone. It is through your love alone. It is through love's perfection that I find you.

1 John 4:18 (TPT) – *"Love never brings fear, for fear is always related to punishment. Love's perfection drives the fear of punishment far from our hearts. Whoever walks constantly afraid of punishment has not reached love's perfection."*

A Passion Translation Footnote – "The immediate context shows that it is the fear of correction, 'punishment,' or rejection. The Aramaic can be translated 'Fear is suspicious.'"

DAY 80

Jesus, I love you completely and wholly. I love you passionately and with such an intensity burning in my heart. I care nothing for what the world offers me. I completely push it aside and push through to see only you. You are Love Himself. You are true love. You are the substance everyone is looking for. You are what I have found. You fill all my needs and all my desires. In the process, you completely saturate me, and I am heavy with the weight of your presence. It is you I carry with me. It isn't something I have picked up in my travels in life. I drop all my baggage and only carry you with me. I don't want what looks good or is impressive to other people. I don't want knowledge that is twisted or tainted.

I want you.

You are the fullest expression of everything I could ever hope for. You are everything I cannot even imagine yet. You are the pinnacle, the highest. I want you with me. I want Love Himself with me. I want to have a life filled with you – all of you in all of me. I want to be seen as so pure, so radiant, so rare, so genuine by those around me – I want them to know I have been with you and that I am continually with you. I love you. I carry you. I am filled and saturated with you. Only you can be my foundation. Only you can be my walls. Only you can be my roof. Only you can fill my house. You are my very structure. You are my contents. You are my dwelling place. You are my secret place. You are my life. You are my love.

1 Corinthians 8:1 (TPT) – "...*But love builds up the structure of our new life.*"

A Passion Translation Footnote – "That is, knowledge may make a person look important, but it is only through love that we reach families, and others. Love is the most powerful substance for building what will last forever."

Day 81

Jesus, I marvel at how you love me. I am completely swept away by how you love me. How can such perfect love be a mystery to me? How can you create such divineness and romance in the essence of love? You are an amazing creator. You designed love so perfectly, and, in its true form, it is pristine in every aspect. I love that you, Jesus, are my bridegroom and that your love for me is so pure. I love how you see me as the one you desire, the one you want, the one you would and did lay it all down for. I want to dedicate myself to you, to tenderly and affectionately love you with everything I have. I put you on the pedestal of my heart. It is you alone that moves me. You cause my heart to beat wildly and to rest so contently. I am forever yours.

You make me smile. You fill all of me. The way you look at me melts me. It sweeps me off my feet. The way your hand feels holding my hand is comforting. I mold myself to you when you put your arms around me. Your voice is unmistakable. I cling to every word you speak. My gaze is always fastened to your face. Just to be with you is what I want. It is all I desire. It drives me. It motivates me. It soothes me. I want you. I want your love — what a mystery. However, the thing I know is that you are mine and I am yours, forever. Love has captured me. Lock me in your arms and never let me go. I marvel at the mystery of love, but I am so captivated and mesmerized by its creator. I love you, Jesus. With all of my heart. With all I am. Forever.

Proverbs 30:18-19 (TPT) – *"There are four marvelous mysteries that are too amazing to unravel – who could fully explain them? ...and the way a bridegroom falls in love with his bride."*

A Passion Translation Footnote – "...More importantly, this is a beautiful metaphor for the mystery of the love of our heavenly Bridegroom (Jesus), who romances his bride and sweeps us off our feet. Love is a mystery."

DAY 82

Jesus, I love you beyond myself and my capacity. I want to please you. I want you to love how I represent you. I want to be your perfect bride, so virtuous and victorious, a reflection of who you are. Pour your love over me and saturate me with your grace so I may be your counterpart, full of virtue. Help me to have strength and endurance so that my role and identity as your bride is fluid and effortless. Let my character be noble and represent your stature. With all I say, with all I do, with all I think, with all I am, cause me to exhaust the limits of your desire and plan for the perfect bride. I want to be lovely in your eyes, filled with inner grace that flows outwardly. I want to be diligent, a steward of talents and gifts you have given me. I want to be full of your knowledge, wisdom, discernment, and prudence. I want to be the one you have created me to be. Let me honor you, my bridegroom, and always make your name great. I love you Jesus, my one and only, my shining and valiant bridegroom, the one who consumes my heart. When you see me, when you think of me, I want you to rejoice that you have found a wife like me. I love you. I love you. I love you.

Proverbs 31:10 (TPT) – *"Who could ever find a wife like this one -* ..."

A Passion Translation Footnote – "Starting with verse 10 through the end of the book, we have a Hebrew acrostic poem. It is alphabetical in structure, with each of the twenty-two verses beginning with a consecutive Hebrew letter of the alphabet. The implication is that the perfections of this woman would exhaust the entire language. The subject is the perfect bride, the virtuous woman. This woman is both a picture of a virtuous wife and an incredible allegory of the end-time victorious bride of Jesus Christ, full of virtue and grace."

DAY 83

Jesus, I love you. You are so wonderful, so amazing, so complete and all I ever need. I am so pleased and so honored to be your bride. Let me fulfill all your expectations and exceed them. I know that your love for me never changes, so nothing I can do will ever increase or decrease your love for me. I don't want to be weak and powerless. I want to emanate all you are from within me. You make me powerful and victorious. You give me power and authority and dominion. I intend on being what you want and what you desire – all you made me to be. I am not a passive bride, but a warring one who is mighty like an army.

Let me make you proud. All these qualities and characteristics are only to point to you, my far exceeding and wonderful bridegroom.

You have made me to be wealthy and excellent, morally righteous, full of substance and integrity. This list of qualities and characteristics is meant to please you and only you. Let everything you desire be found in me. Let no one be found with a higher quality of these – for I am set apart – to love you and please only you. You are all these things, and you dwell in me. You reign in me. Therefore, in my love for you, let me be the wife of noble character, let me be the one, the true one, that unreservedly cherishes, adores, and loves you in quality, character, and all else.

Proverbs 31:10 (TPT) – *"...she is a woman of strength and valor! She's full of wealth and wisdom..."*

A Passion Translation Footnote – "The Hebrew word used to describe this virtuous wife is *"khayil."* The meaning of this word cannot be contained by one English equivalent word. It is often used in connection with military prowess. This is a warring wife. *Khayil* can be translated 'mighty; wealthy; excellent; morally righteous; full of substance, integrity, abilities, and strength; mighty like an army.' The wife is a metaphor for the last-days church, the virtuous, overcoming bride of Jesus Christ. The word *khayil* is most often used to describe valiant men… where it is used for the mighty ones, Moses was to commission as elders and leaders among the people…"

Day 84

Jesus, thank you for being such a sweet and precious Bridegroom. Thank you for being so extraordinary, so far surpassing any other. Thank you for your eternal love, your perfect love, that is all for me. Thank you that you are Love Himself and that you always think about me. Your thoughts were always toward me since before the foundation of the earth. You prepared yourself in advance, knowing I would need to be rescued and redeemed. You knew the price that would need to be paid for me. You love me like no other. I am so amazed and so in awe of you. You are so exceptional, so pure, so perfect. You are the only one that could pay the price for me – and it was you. You were that very price. You are blameless. You are spotless. You are radiant. You saw me as your joy. Even in my imperfection, in my lowness, in my separation from you, you still loved me as you always have and always will. Your love was steadfast. Your love was so genuine and pure. You are truly the one for me. I am the one for you. You paid the price for me. You gave your life so I can have life. I give you my life back - all of me. I love you. I am so glad, so thankful, so in love with you.

Proverbs 31:10 (TPT) – *"...The price paid for her was greater than many jewels."*

A Passion Translation Footnote – "Or 'her worth.' The price paid for her was the sacred blood of the Lamb of God, her Bridegroom."

Day 85

I love you, Jesus. You are my heart; you give life to my soul. There is no one like you, no one higher than you, no one more inexpressible than you. You satisfy me. You fill me. You comfort me. You chose me. How thrilling it is for me to be your bride. I can't hide my excitement. I must shout it from the rooftops. I love that I am the one you have chosen because you are the One I want. I want to be worthy of being your counterpart. I want to make you proud. Your love fills me, and because of your love, I am strengthened and able to be the bride you have imagined. I want to know you deeper and deeper. Reveal your heart to me; I want to know your heart. I want the innermost parts of your heart to melt into mine. If I don't have your heart, I don't have you. I take pleasure in knowing you. I am the bride that you lift up. I am the overcoming bride, the victorious bride. I can only do this because you are mine and I am yours. I want to bring you the rich spoils of victory because you have entrusted me with your heart.

Proverbs 31:11 (TPT) – *"Her husband has entrusted his heart to her, for she brings him the rich spoils of victory."*

Day 86

Jesus, I love you. I love everything about you. I love all of you. I love your face. Your eyes pull me in day after day and allow me to see your heart and soul. I get drawn deeper and more fully into you so that I know you like no one else. The beauty that I see, the glory that I see, is beyond my expression. You are so pure, so pristine, and so absolute. I want your purity. I seek purity. I desire to possess purity in all things. I stand before you as the one who loves you and adores you. Thank you that I can stand before you in righteousness. Thank you that I have right-standing before you – not because of anything I have done, but because of everything you have done. My heart beats deep and wide and high and low for you. My attire is only wool and linen before you. I am adorned with your love and grace. When you see me, I want you to see nothing but one completely and desperately devoted to you – loving you in purity and righteousness.

Proverbs 31:13 (TPT) – *"She searches out continually to possess that which is pure and righteous…"*

A Passion Translation Footnote – "Or 'wool and linen [flax].' Wool is a metaphor often used as a symbol of what is pure…Linen was made from flax and always speaks of righteousness. The priests of the Old Testament wore linen garments as they went before God's presence to offer sacrifices. The curtains of the tabernacle were likewise made of linen, signifying God's righteousness… The virtuous bride of Christ in the last days will be seeking for only what is pure and righteous in the eyes of her Bridegroom."

DAY 87

Jesus, I thank you that I can love you. I am in awe of my position as your bride and that I get to fill my life with you. You are everything to me. You are my all. I don't want anything without you. What you give me is divine; you supply me with everything I need or ever will need. You provide overflow for me so that I can share your goodness with others. You are my source for everything. You give me provision. You fill me with good and perfect containers of your grace. Your provision never runs out; it never runs dry; it never ends. There is no lack in you. You are the abundance of love. You paid for my supply to be full. You purchased my provision. You purchased me. It was your life, your spotless and sacred blood, that was the price for me. You showed me, true love. Your love was not selfish, or deficient in any way. Your love was sacrificial. Your love gave all it had for me. You are the merchant that loads precious cargo for me. This cargo is precious; it is satisfying; it is comforting. It is you. You are the cargo that I want. You are the source. You are the substance. You are the end and the means. You are life. You – only you – can be all to me.

Proverbs 31:14 (TPT) – *"...She is like a trading ship bringing divine supplies from the merchant."*

A Passion Translation Footnote – "Or 'like merchant ships bringing goods.' Like a ship loaded with cargo, the bride of Christ brings heavenly treasures to others. The use of the term merchant points to Jesus Christ. He is described as a merchant in Matt. 13:45 in the parable of the costly pearl. The 'pearl' is the church or the believer, which cost all that Jesus had (his blood) to purchase us."

DAY 88

Jesus, I love you. Thank you for being with me in all seasons. Thank you that you are with me in the day and night. You are with me on the mountain and in the valley. You are with me in every moment of my life. I am never alone because you are always with me. When the darkness comes, I obey and arise. I rise in power as your bride. I am not left defenseless or without power. I have your power in me because I am yours. There is always provision for me and my household. There is also overflow with which we can bless others. I shine with your love to those around me because your light illumines my soul. My light has come. I am no longer in darkness. You are the light. Where you are, there is no darkness. As your bride, I rise and shine to feed and bless others. This is my role. This is my task. This comes from my identity as your counterpart. You have given me all I need. You have provided a way for me. It is because of you, the one I love, that I can rise and shine, with power, when darkness comes. Your light comes and is with me. It dispels darkness. Your light invades my space. Your grace invades my soul. Your love rescues me continually. Your love causes me to be victorious. You alone. It is you alone.

Proverbs 31:15 (TPT) – *"Even in the night season she arises and sets food on the table for hungry ones in her house and others."*

A Passion Translation Footnote – "The Hebrew word translated *'arise'* can also mean 'to rise in power.' We are told to 'arise and shine, for our light has come.' See Isaiah 60:1, which uses the same Hebrew word for *'arise.'* The bride of Christ will arise with anointing to feed and bless the people of God."

DAY 89

Jesus, you are so beautiful. You are so good. You are so precious. You are mine. How can I express just what you are? You are beyond the capability of my language. I can use words to tell you how good you are, how worthy you are, how much I love you, but I will never be able to fully communicate that. My comfort is that you know my heart. I'm so glad that you know every part of me. You know my thoughts, my intentions, my wishes, desires. You know my joys and my hurts. You know my sincerity and the depths of my surrender to you. You know what I mean even before I say it. You know my heart before I act. I want you to be proud of me. I never want to disappoint you. I only want to honor you and love you. Be so pleased with me, Jesus. I want every word that you speak about me to be good ones, proud ones, glowing ones. Your words about me are always promises and truth.

Your words are always "Yes" to me. My heart smiles knowing that I am always yours and that your love for me is steadfast and eternal. Even if I fall short, your love does not waver. It is strong. You love me with a fierceness that was proven by your sacrifice for me – your very life. You delivered me. You redeemed me. I am such a grateful bride, full of love for you. Your words about me give me encouragement to never stop. Your praise of me lifts me; it fills me with power. You are the Word, and when you speak of me, you speak yourself to me. You speak yourself over me. You speak life into me. You speak all your promises to me. I cling to every word you speak.

Jesus, you fill me and love me. You are so amazing. I love you. I am so proud to love you. I am so happy to love you. I am too honored to love you. I could step away from all there is to do in this life and love you. Only you.

Proverbs 31:28 (TPT) — *"...and her husband arises to speak of her in glowing terms."*

DAY 90

Jesus, I love you every day. I love you today. I will love you tomorrow. My heart has turned to love because it is filled with only love. You have exceeded my hopes. You have surpassed my desires. No one else could ever be like you. You are so pure, so spotless, and so radiant. You are the source of all things. You are the answer to all things. You are everything to me. You are. You make me special. You make me great. You make me righteous. You forgive me. You heal me. You take away my grief. You take away all my sickness and disease. You give me a hope and a future. You give me an identity. You give me a purpose. You fill me with love. You cover me with grace. You created me. You make me who I am. You continue to mold me into what I am to be. I am your joy. I am the one you love. I was always at the center of your thoughts and the reason for your love. What a mystery! What love! What an epic love story of the ages. I am the valiant and noble one you love, your bride. You raise me high. I will spend eternity going deeper and deeper into you, loving you more and more. I don't know how it will be possible to love you more, but from where I have been to where I am now, I have confidence that this is just the beginning.

Proverbs 31:29 (TPT) – *"There are many valiant and noble ones, but you have ascended above them all!"*

A Passion Translation Footnote – "Or 'You are first in his eyes...'"

ABOUT THE AUTHOR

Based on Faith was founded by Crystal G.H. Lowery in 2012. Crystal is also the principle and founding attorney of Law Office of Crystal G.H. Lowery, LLC, a firm dedicated to estate planning, elder law, Veteran planning, business planning, and entertainment law.

The ministry was formed as a response to what Crystal saw and experienced in her law practice. Crystal enjoyed practicing law in a positive and creative way. However, she consistently experienced a lack of knowledge in the general population, even with those clients she worked with who were professing Christians. The knowledge gap that she recognized was two-fold. One aspect was just relating to factual information relating to law and faith. The second aspect was integration of law and faith.

Crystal began to speak to various groups and organizations as well to teach courses relating to estate planning. However, more and more she became uncomfortable and disturbed by the traditional teaching and wisdom of estate planners and financial planners. She saw the fear in the eyes of precious people when they asked questions and wondered if they were making the right decisions. This prompted Crystal to take a good hard look at the subject and do something different, something more in line with what the word of God teaches. Crystal looked at her process and at each step along the way in the decision-making process and evaluated it according to faith-based principles. What she found was more and more inspiring each time.

The subject matter she practiced influenced all aspects of one's life and family and as a matter of desperation, must be looked at from the correct lens. The desire to share this information was so overwhelming that Crystal founded *Based on Faith*. Based on Faith began simply from Crystal writing relevant articles she shared twice a week on the *Based on Faith Blog*. The response she received was very affirming in that people were searching for answers.

Crystal speaks to groups, organizations, and churches as well as continues to write. The goal is to shed light on darkness. A common quotation we hear is that we can't expect for anything different to happen if we keep doing the same thing. This is what *Based on Faith* strives to do – to inspire and help people to think and live differently from traditional or orthodox patterns. Based on Faith is excited by the necessity of an opportunity to fill a gap to help people. Based on Faith uses personal methods and cutting-edge technology to share its message, but the message remains the same – it is *Based on Faith*.

Crystal earned a B.A. in Communications with an emphasis in Public Relations from Virginia Tech, and earned a M.A. in Communications with an emphasis in Producing and Directing for Film and Television from Regent University School of Communications and the Arts. In addition, she earned a J.D. from Regent University School of Law.

Crystal is a mother of one daughter and three sons. Being their mom is one of the greatest blessings in her life. Crystal was married to her husband, Kevin, for almost 17 years until he went to be with Jesus in 2018.

Crystal G.H. Lowery
P.O. Box 410
Isle of Palms, SC 29466

Website: www.basedonfaith.org

Email: info@basedonfaith.org

Your financial support of this non-profit 501(c)3 ministry is appreciated.

$ 388.00
28 -5
9:3

CPSIA information can be obtained
at www.ICGtesting.com
Printed in the USA
BVHW042047310819
557323BV00017B/850/P